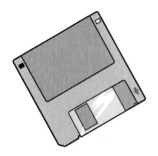

Installation Instructions for America Online Disk

Installing and using America Online for Windows version 2.5 is easy. The following steps will get you started online with AOL using the disk packaged with this book.

1. Insert the disk included with this book in your disk drive (**A** or **B**).

2. Select **Run** from the **File** menu of your Windows Program Manager, type **A:\SETUP** (or **B:\SETUP**), and click on **OK**. Then click on **Install** to install your software in the indicated directory.

3. Once installation is complete, click on **OK,** double-click on the **America Online** icon, and follow the simple step-by-step instructions on your screen. When prompted, enter the **registration number** and **password** included with your disk.

The disk included with this book is for IBM-PCs or compatibles. If you need a Macintosh disk, please return the PC disk to us at the address below and request that a disk for use on the Macintosh be sent to you.

Disk Exchange
Ziff-Davis Press
5903 Christie Avenue
Emeryville, CA 94608

How to Use

AMERICA ONLINE

SECOND EDITION

How to Use

AMERICA ONLINE

SECOND EDITION

ELAINE MADISON

Illustrated by
SARAH ISHIDA

Que New Technologies
Emeryville, California

Editor	Margo R. Hill
Technical Reviewer	Mark Hall
Project Coordinator	Nicole Clausing
Proofreader	Jeff Barash
Cover Design and Illustration	Regan Honda
Book Design	Dennis Gallagher/Visual Strategies,San Francisco
Screen Graphics Editor	P. Diamond
Technical Illustration	Sarah Ishida
Word Processing	Howard Blechman
Page Layout	Meredith Downs and Dana Goforth
Indexer	Kayla Sussel

Ziff-Davis Press, ZD Press, and the Ziff-Davis Press logo are licensed to Macmillan Computer Publishing USA by Ziff-Davis Publishing Company, New York, New York.

Ziff-Davis Press imprint books are produced on a Macintosh computer system with the following applications: FrameMaker®, Microsoft® Word, QuarkXPress®, Adobe Illustrator®, Adobe Photoshop®, Adobe Streamline™, MacLink® *Plus*, Aldus® FreeHand™, Collage Plus™.

If you have comments or questions or would like to receive a free catalog, call or write:
Macmillan Computer Publishing USA
Ziff-Davis Press Line of Books
5903 Christie Avenue
Emeryville, CA 94608
800-688-0448

ISBN 1-56276-349-0

Manufactured in the United States of America
10 9 8 7 6 5 4 3 2 1

*To my friends and
family for always
supporting my new
adventures.*

TABLE OF CONTENTS

INTRODUCTION

 You're new to America Online and its companion communications program, America Online for Windows. Maybe you're not quite sure what an online service is or what a communications program does. Maybe you've never even used a computer before. You're not looking to become an expert. You don't need hotshot shortcuts. You just want to see how this online thing works.

How to Use America Online, Second Edition is for you. This concise, colorful book includes an America Online for Windows version 2.5 software disk so you can get online today. Once online we'll take you on a guided tour, during which you'll see how to tap into America Online's many treasures—right before your eyes, step by step, topic by topic. When you're done reading this book, you'll be a comfortable, confident America Online member. From games and electronic mail to online news and the legendary Internet, the power and fun of online information will be right at your fingertips.

Each chapter in this book presents several related topics. Because each topic fits in a section spanning just two facing pages, everything you need to know about that topic is in front of you at one time. Just follow the numbered steps around the pages, reading the text and looking at the pictures. It's really as easy as it looks!

Colorful, realistic examples are included to help you understand your options for using America Online. You can work along as you learn, but that's not mandatory. If you want to stay focused on your own information needs and use this book just as a reference, you'll find it well suited to that purpose.

Even experienced computer users occasionally stumble into unfamiliar territory. Read the "Tip Sheet" accompanying each topic to learn more about related pitfalls or about alternative methods for accomplishing the task at hand.

You also will find three special sections called "Try It!" at strategic spots in this book. Each Try It! section is a hands-on exercise that gives you valuable practice with some of the skills you've acquired to that point. As you read a Try It! section, be sure to follow each step at your computer.

To get the most value out of this book, read Chapters 1 through 11 in sequence. These chapters will help you get familiar with features like e-mail and downloading and terms you'll use in later chapters which discuss America Online's departments. If you already have some experience with America Online, or with online services and computers in general, you may be familiar with the information in the first two chapters. Skimming these chapters, however, can provide a useful refresher on major concepts and terminology.

Note: This book was specifically designed for America Online for Windows with Windows 95, but works almost equally as well with Windows version 3.1 or Windows for Workgroups version 3.11. Users should notice only a few minor differences in the appearance of their screens using the other Windows versions.

CHAPTER 1

What Is an Online Service?

An *online service*, from a technical point of view, is a commercial telecommunications system that provides a way for your computer to connect to other computers for the purpose of exchanging information. It's a *telecommunications system* because you communicate with the service by means of ordinary telephone lines. It's a *commercial service* because you pay money so that the service provider can make a profit.

From a more personal aspect, an online service is the world at your fingertips. With an online service, you can get the latest news and weather reports, check out how your favorite sports team did last night, read a couple of jokes, send a message to a friend halfway around the world, order a pair of plane tickets, and ask a complete stranger for advice—all without getting up from your computer.

This book teaches you how to use one online service, America Online, which is widely regarded as one of the most graphical and easiest to use services around. Read on to find out why.

America Online Is Your Online Service

America Online isn't the only online service available. Just as different banks serve the various financial needs of any community, there are more than a few online services to serve the information needs of the nation and the world. As with banks, all online services offer the same basic features, but each does so with a unique emphasis. Services such as CompuServe focus on the needs of businesses and experienced computer users. Others, America Online included, tend to serve more personal needs. This isn't to say that you can't use CompuServe to meet some personal needs, or America Online to address business issues—it's simply a matter of focus.

TIP SHEET

▸ **This book is about using the America Online for Windows version 2.5 software to connect to America Online. Unless you have the right software, you cannot be sure that everything you read in this book applies to you. Look on your installation disk(s) for the number 2.5 and the phrase *for Windows*; if you find you have the wrong disk(s), call America Online (1-800-827-6364) and ask for a free replacement.**

▸ **Your modem may be internal (hidden inside your computer's main case) or external (a small box sitting outside the case). If you're not sure whether you have a modem, check with the vendor who sold you your computer, or ask a computer-savvy friend.**

▸ **Chapter 2 of this book is for first-time computer users or first-time Windows users. If you're already using Windows 95 and know how to use your mouse, issue menu commands, and select dialog box options, you can skip ahead to Chapter 3. If you don't know what these operations are, or if you need to review them, then Chapter 2 is just for you.**

▶ **1** America Online consists of two basic components: the *service* and the *communications software*. To keep things straight, we'll refer to the service, or the service and software collectively, as *America Online*. When we talk specifically about the software, we'll say *America Online for Windows*. (More about Windows in a moment.)

7 What makes America Online so popular? Well, it's easy to learn, easy to use, relatively fast, and supplies information from many different arenas. As a new user, you'll appreciate the ease of use; as you work with America Online more and more, you'll come to appreciate its speed and diversity.

6 America Online is well regarded by many computer users. You'll be using an online service and communications software that have withstood the test of time and acquired hundreds of thousands of faithful members.

2 America Online, the service, is headquartered in Vienna, Virginia (a suburb of Arlington, just outside Washington, D.C.). It's a set of computers—collectively known as *The Stratus* by people who like to name computers—that contains loads of information ready for the taking. This information is constantly updated so that when you check something such as a news report, you can be sure that you're getting the most recent information.

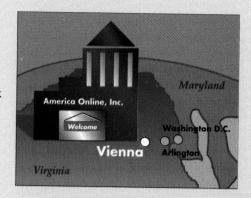

3 America Online for Windows, the software, re-sides on the hard disks of computers that are set up to connect to America Online. Just as a CD player needs CDs to make music, each computer needs software to tell it what to do. America Online for Windows tells your computer how to connect to America Online. (Computers can be set up to run all types of software, including word processors, spreadsheets, databases, and games.) You'll learn how to set up America Online for Windows on your computer in Chapter 3.

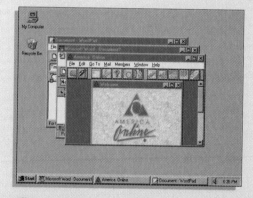

4 As the name implies, America Online for Windows is software that is based on *Microsoft Windows*, a program that con-trols, among other things, the "look" of your computer screen. The America Online for Windows *interface* (that is, the way you give commands to the software and receive information from it) is similar to that of other Windows-based software, including some you may already know how to use. (More about Windows in Chapter 2.)

5 To make the connection between your computer and the ones in Virginia, you use ordinary telephone lines. Because telephone lines are designed for human voices rather than computer infor-mation, your computer must have a special piece of equipment called a *modem* (short for *modulator/demodulator*) to translate the computer information traveling to and from your computer.

CHAPTER 2

Getting Acquainted with Windows

 Windows is a program (the terms program and software are used interchangeably here) that enables you to run the programs you really want to run: your communications software (America Online for Windows), your word processor, your games, and so on. If you are using Windows 95, which this book is based on, it is also your computer's operating system, coordinating the operations of all the parts in your computer system.

Windows simplifies your role in directing your computer. It also provides a consistent and appealing backdrop for all Windows-based software. Windows-based programs look comfortingly similar on the screen and there are many similarities in the way you work with these programs.

If you are using Windows 95, "windows" starts automatically whenever you turn on your computer. This chapter helps you use Windows.

How to Start a Program from the Desktop

The desktop is the large area you see when you start Windows. Its role is to make it easy for you to start other programs and manage your work. Like your own desktop at work or home it can be customized to fit your mood or personality; you can even put your favorite pictures on it.

▶ **1** Start on the Desktop provides you with immediate access to programs. The Start button opens a menu with items to let you find files and programs, change your Windows settings, access help, run programs and even shut down your computer. Click once on the Start button and everything on your computer is just a mouse click away.

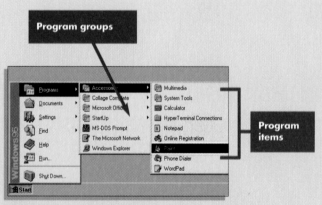

6 So how do all these elements work together? When you want to start a program, first click the Start button and point to Programs on the Start menu. If the program does not appear on the continuation menu, point to the program group (or folder) that contains the desired program item. For instance, to open the program Paint, move the mouse pointer from Programs to the Accessories group (or folder), point to the Paint program item icon, and click.

TIP SHEET

▶ To close an application or document window, click on the Window menu box in the window's upper-left corner (or click once on the box and then click on Close).

▶ Once a program has been started, a button appears on the taskbar. To switch from running one program to another, click the button on the taskbar.

▶ If you can't find the program in the Programs menu, point to Find on the Start menu, and click Files or Folders. Use the Find dialog box to locate the program (dialog boxes are covered later in this chapter).

2 Moving through the Start menu is as easy as moving your mouse; just move the mouse pointer from one item to the next. Menu items with an arrowhead next to them are Continuation menus; just point to the item and another menu will open. No clicking necessary!

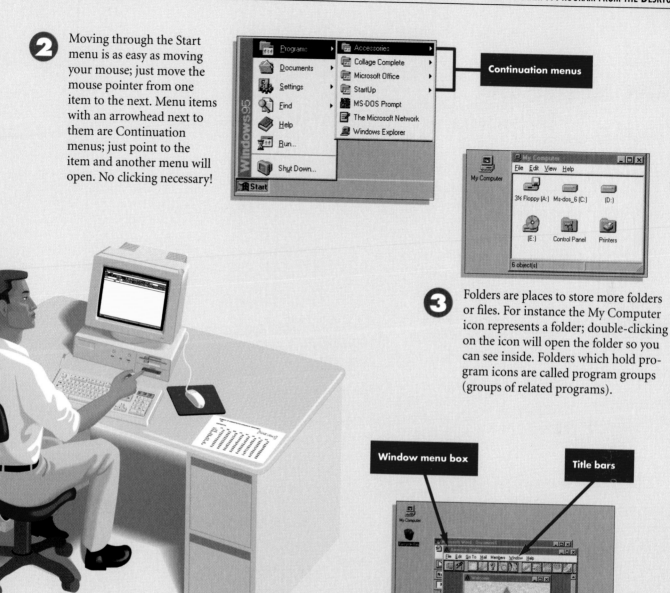

3 Folders are places to store more folders or files. For instance the My Computer icon represents a folder; double-clicking on the icon will open the folder so you can see inside. Folders which hold program icons are called program groups (groups of related programs).

Continuation menus

Window menu box

Title bars

Taskbar

Minimized windows

Active window

5 The taskbar, which also holds the Start button, keeps track of all the windows you have open: minimized, hidden, or active. You'll always know what's running by checking the taskbar.

4 You can have zero, one, or multiple windows open at one time, but only one window can be active. The active window is the one affected by the commands you issue. Every window contains a title bar, which displays the name of the program or document in that window. The title bar of the active window will always be a different color or shade than the title bars of inactive windows.

How to Use the Mouse in Windows

An *input device* is a means of giving instructions to your computer. You may be familiar with the keyboard as the most common input device. A *mouse*, so named for its size and tail-like cable, is a hand-held input device that, along with the keyboard, is one of the two input devices typically used in Windows. Take a few minutes to learn the major mouse techniques, and your efforts will pay off handsomely.

Arrow   I-beam

▶ **1** Grab your mouse with the "tail" pointing away from you and your fingers resting over the buttons, and then move the mouse around on your mouse pad or desktop. As you do, the on-screen *mouse pointer* moves in synch with the mouse. Usually, the mouse pointer appears as either an arrow or an I-beam. Because you use the mouse to point, mice are sometimes called *pointing devices*.

▶ It takes some practice to become efficient with a mouse, especially when double-clicking and dragging. Be patient; you'll feel like an expert in no time.

▶ Some mice have two buttons, and others have three. The left mouse button is the most commonly used, for opening menus, dragging, pointing, and so on. The right mouse button opens a menu with available options specific to where you clicked in the window. The middle mouse button is almost never used unless you have a special mouse program to take advantage of it.

▶ Mice are not the only pointing devices available. If your computer is equipped with some other type of pointing device, such as a trackball or pointing stick, you can use that instead of a mouse.

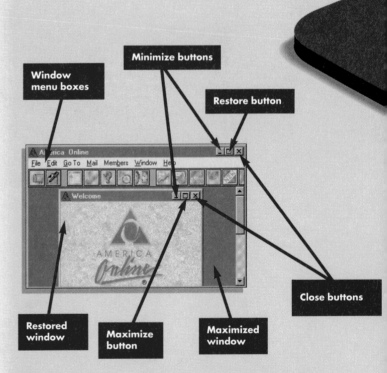

Window menu boxes

Minimize buttons

Restore button

Close buttons

Restored window

Maximize button

Maximized window

6 To *maximize* a window (that is, to enlarge it so that the window fills the entire screen), click on the window's *Maximize button*. To *restore* a maximized window to its previous size, click on the window's *Restore button* (which will appear in place of the Maximize button). To *minimize* a window to the task bar, click on the window's *Minimize button*. To restore a minimized window to its previous size, click on the icon in the task bar.

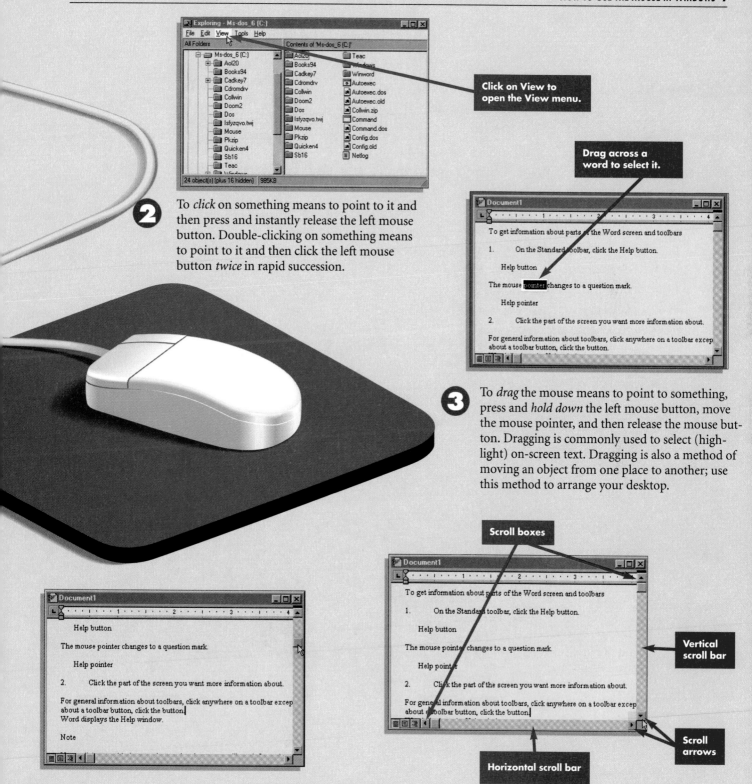

Click on View to open the View menu.

Drag across a word to select it.

2 To *click* on something means to point to it and then press and instantly release the left mouse button. Double-clicking on something means to point to it and then click the left mouse button *twice* in rapid succession.

3 To *drag* the mouse means to point to something, press and *hold down* the left mouse button, move the mouse pointer, and then release the mouse button. Dragging is commonly used to select (highlight) on-screen text. Dragging is also a method of moving an object from one place to another; use this method to arrange your desktop.

Scroll boxes

Vertical scroll bar

Horizontal scroll bar

Scroll arrows

5 Another way to scroll is to drag the *scroll box* to a new location on the *scroll bar*. The position of the scroll box suggests what part of the window's contents you are viewing. For example, when the scroll box is in about the middle of the vertical scroll bar, you are about halfway down from the top of the window contents.

4 When a window or window element contains too much information to be viewed all at once, point to one of the *scroll arrows* and hold down the left mouse button to *scroll* through the display in the direction of the arrow.

How to Use the Keyboard in Windows

In Windows and most Windows-based programs, you don't have to use the keyboard for much of anything—except, of course, to type text. But if you do quite a bit of typing, you may be interested in optional ways to scroll through windows, issue commands, and perform other common actions *without* having to reach for the mouse. The more you work with Windows, the more you may yearn for keyboard alternatives to mouse actions that seem inconvenient to you. Even if you're a true "mouse-o-phile," you should be aware of the major keyboard techniques in case your mouse ever malfunctions.

TIP SHEET

▶ In many programs, the Page Up and Page Down keys (sometimes labeled PgUp and PgDn) scroll the window in large increments. Ctrl+Home often moves you to the beginning of a window's contents, and Ctrl+End often moves you to the end.

▶ Your keyboard may not look exactly like the one pictured here, especially if your keyboard is a few years old or if you're using a small, portable computer. All keyboards, however, share essentially the same set of keys. If you have trouble finding the keys described here, check the documentation that came with your computer.

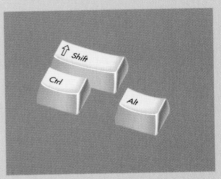

▶ **1** The Shift, Alt, and Ctrl keys almost always work in combination with other keys. You probably know that holding down the Shift key as you press a letter key produces a capital letter. The Alt and Ctrl keys work the same way, but the results depend on the program you are using at the time.

7 The Escape key (labeled Esc on most keyboards) lets you back out of many potentially hazardous situations. If you open a menu, but decide not to issue a command, press Escape twice to close the menu and deactivate the menu bar. If you issue a command and a dialog box opens, but you don't want to proceed, press Escape once to close the dialog box. (Dialog boxes are described on the next page.)

2 The Shift, Alt, and Ctrl keys are often combined with the *function keys*—labeled F1 through F10, F12, or F16—to issue commands. For example, you can close most Windows programs by pressing Alt+F4 (hold down Alt, press and release F4, and then release Alt). The function keys can also work alone. The function keys are usually located in the keyboard's top row (as shown here) or along the keyboard's left side.

3 When you don't want to reach for the mouse to scroll through the contents of a window, use the ↑, ↓, ←, and → *arrow keys* instead. Many keyboards contain *two* sets of arrow keys. Arrow keys that display just arrows always work as arrow keys. Arrow keys that display both arrows and numbers, however, are dual-purpose keys; they can work as arrow keys *or* as number keys. To toggle these dual-purpose keys, use the Num Lock key.

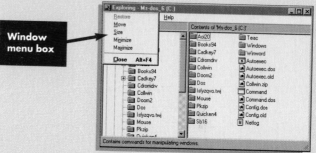

Window menu box

4 Another way to maximize, minimize, restore, or close a window is through its Window menu box. Press Alt+Spacebar to open an application window's Window menu bar; press Alt+hyphen to open a document's Window menu box. Use the ↓ key to highlight the command you want: Maximize, Minimize, Restore, or Close. Then press Enter.

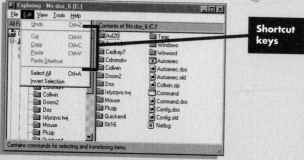

Shortcut keys

6 Many menus also list keyboard alternatives (shortcut keys) right next to their most frequently used commands. Although these shortcut keys work only when the menu is closed, the listing serves as a reminder for next time.

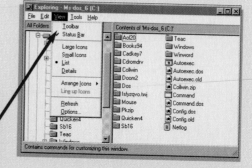

Type the underlined character to select the menu item and issue the command.

5 To open a menu from the menu bar, hold down Alt, type the underlined character in the menu name (for example, F for File or V for View), and then release Alt. To select an item from an open menu, use the ↓ and Enter keys as described in step 4, or simply type the item's underlined character.

How to Talk to a Dialog Box

A *dialog box* is basically an on-screen questionnaire where you provide the extra information a program needs to carry out a command you have issued. For example, say you issue the File, Print command, which is available in many Windows-based programs. Before printing anything, however, the program will open a dialog box to ask you how much of the current window contents to print, how many copies to print, what printer to use, and so on. Once you answer these questions, the command is executed.

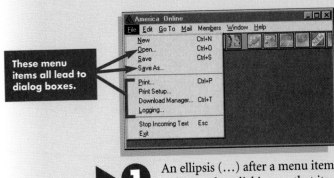

These menu items all lead to dialog boxes.

1 An ellipsis (...) after a menu item indicates that clicking on that item will open a dialog box.

Radio buttons

OK

7 When you've provided all the requested information in a dialog box, click on the *OK button*, or on another of the available *command buttons*. (The button names will be Print, Find, or something else related to the command.)

TIP SHEET

▶ To choose a dialog-box option using the keyboard, press and hold down Alt, type the option's underlined character, and then release Alt. If the option doesn't have an underlined character, press Tab to move from one option to the next. Then, to check or uncheck a check box, press the spacebar. To mark a radio button within a group, use the arrow keys. To open a drop-down list, press ↓ or Alt+↓; press ↓ as needed to highlight your choice, and then press Tab.

▶ If you need to see what's behind a dialog box, move the box by dragging its title bar.

▶ To close a dialog box without executing the command, click on the Cancel button (available in most dialog boxes), double-click on the dialog box's Control Menu box, or press Esc.

▶ Sometimes a menu item or a dialog-box option is *dimmed*. This means the option is not currently available.

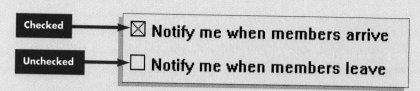

Checked

Unchecked

2 One way to answer a dialog-box question is to check or uncheck a *check box*. Click in an empty check box to check it; an X fills the box to show that the option is active. Click in a checked check box to turn off the option; the X disappears.

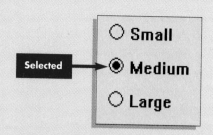

Selected

3 Sometimes dialog-box options are grouped as *radio buttons* (also known as *option buttons*). You can select (activate) only one radio button within a group at one time, and at least one button must be selected at all times. Select a radio button by clicking on it; the previously selected button automatically clears. It works just like the station-selector buttons on old-style car radios—hence the name.

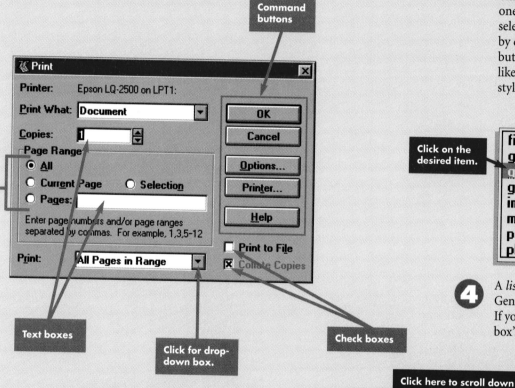

Command buttons

Text boxes

Click for drop-down box.

Check boxes

Click on the desired item.

4 A *list box* displays a list of choices. Generally, you can select only one choice. If your choice isn't visible, use the list box's scroll bar to scroll through the list.

Click here to scroll down through the drop-down list.

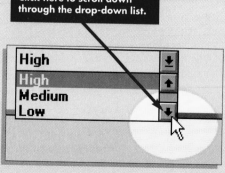

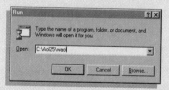

6 To enter or change text in a *text box*, first click anywhere in the box. Then use the arrow keys to position the *insertion point* (the flashing vertical bar), use the Backspace and Delete keys to delete the existing text as needed, and then type new text from the keyboard.

5 A down-pointing arrow with a line below it means you can click on the arrow to see a *drop-down list* of choices. When you spot your choice, click on it. If your choice isn't visible, use the list's scroll bar.

CHAPTER 3

Welcome to America Online

Before you can enjoy all that America Online has to offer, you need to install America Online for Windows on your computer. Once that's done, you can start the software and use it to connect to America Online in Virginia. This may sound like a fairly complex process, but it isn't. The people at America Online who designed the service and its software have already taken the time to establish all the esoteric variables of online communications, such as baud rate, stop bits, parity, and file transfer protocols. All you need to do is issue a few commands and provide some information about yourself. The software and the service do the rest.

Important: Before proceeding any further, be sure that your computer is equipped with a modem, that the modem is in good working order, and that the modem is properly connected to your computer and to an active telephone outlet. If you are unfamiliar with modems, you might want to ask a computer-savvy friend or family member to check out your modem setup for you. *America Online for Windows will not work properly if your modem is not set up properly.*

How to Install America Online for Windows

After turning on your computer, the basic installation procedure is simple: You place an installation disk in your floppy-disk drive, issue a command, and answer a few basic questions. Then your computer copies the appropriate information from the installation disk to your computer's hard disk. Depending on the speed of your computer, the entire process should take only a few minutes.

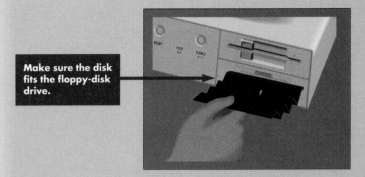

Make sure the disk fits the floppy-disk drive.

▶ **1** Your copy of America Online for Windows is on one or more 3½-inch or 5¼-inch floppy disks. To hold these disks during installation, your computer may have one 3½-inch floppy-disk drive, one 5¼-inch floppy-disk drive, two drives of the same size, or—the most convenient arrangement—one drive of each size. If your installation disks don't fit any of your floppy-disk drives, call America Online at 1-800-827-6364 for a free replacement.

TIP SHEET

▶ **Some computers are sold with America Online for Windows already installed. If your computer already contains an America Online program group and program item, skip ahead to the next page.**

▶ **If you don't have any installation disks at all, there are several ways to get some. The quickest but most expensive method is to go to a computer store and buy one. A slower but much less expensive alternative is to call America Online at 1-800-827-6364 and ask them to send you a free disk (or disks).**

▶ **Although the America Online installation program is designed to work flawlessly, problems do sometimes occur. If you experience a problem during installation, don't panic—the worst that will happen is that you'll have to start over. If you get completely stuck, call America Online for help at 1-800-827-6364.**

▶ **As soon as the installation is finished, you can start America Online for Windows and connect to America Online. Turn the page to see how.**

8 Finally, a dialog box opens to tell you that the installation is complete. Click on OK to close the dialog box and return to the Desktop. There, you'll see a new program group window, entitled America Online, containing the America Online program item. (You'll also find this new program group listed under Programs on the Start menu.)

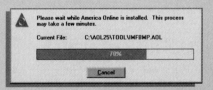

7 Sit back as the installation program copies information from the installation disk to your hard drive. If you are installing from multiple disks, you'll be asked to insert the other disk(s) when appropriate.

Drive A

Drive B

2 You need to know the *drive letter* of the floppy-disk drive you'll be using to install America Online for Windows. If your computer has only one floppy-disk drive, then it is drive A. If your computer has two floppy-disk drives, then the top or left drive is probably drive A, and the bottom or right drive is probably drive B.

3 If you have only one installation disk, insert it in the appropriately sized floppy-disk drive. If you have multiple installation disks, insert the disk labeled Disk 1. **Important:** To be sure you're installing a version of America Online for Windows that will work well with this book, check your installation disk(s) for the number *2.5* and the phrase *for Windows*.

4 Click the Start button on your Desktop and choose Run from the Start menu.

6 After a few moments, the America Online installation program starts, and opens a dialog box to welcome you. Click on Install.

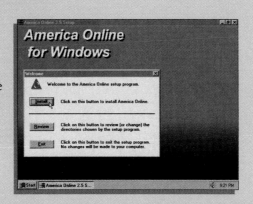

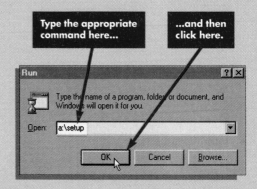

Type the appropriate command here...

...and then click here.

5 Next, a dialog box entitled Run opens. In the Command Line text box, type **a:\setup** if the installation disk is in drive A, or **b:\setup** if the disk is in drive B. Then click on the OK button (or press the Enter key).

How to Sign On to America Online for the First Time

When you start America Online (AOL) for Windows for the first time, the software automatically guides you through the process of *signing on* (connecting) to AOL. This process is fairly automated; however, you should make some preparations ahead of time. First, locate the registration number and password that came with your installation disks. Second, decide how you're going to pay for your AOL membership (VISA, checking account, and so on), and have that information ready. Finally, pick out several *screen names* for yourself. A screen name is a unique nickname of 3 to 10 characters (including spaces) that you use to identify yourself to AOL; having several names ready is helpful in case your first choice is not available.

TIP SHEET

▶ **Because AOL is constantly changing, your computer screen may differ from the ones shown here. Just read each message carefully, and everything will probably work just fine.**

▶ **When choosing a password (step 6), be sure to specify one that you'll remember, but that no one else is likely to guess. Of course, your password's no good if *you* don't remember it, so write it down and put it in a safe place.**

▶ **Traditionally, AOL gives every new member 10 hours of free connect time (starting the moment you see the Welcome! window in step 7) and one month of free membership. As you sign on for the first time, though, be sure to read each message carefully to see what you're getting for free, and how much things are going to cost after that.**

▶ **To learn how to disconnect from AOL, turn the page.**

▶ **①** Click Start, point to Programs, point to the America Online program group, and click on the America Online program item. (See Chapter 2 if you need help with these operations.)

7 After working your way through that long parade of dialog boxes and windows, you'll finally see a Welcome! window similar to this one. You are now successfully signed on to the AOL service for the first time!

6 Continue to read and carefully follow the on-screen directions. You'll first be asked to provide some personal information (name, address, and so on). Then you'll be given some information on the cost of AOL membership, asked to select a billing method (VISA, MasterCard, American Express, Discover, or your checking account) and enter the necessary information about that method; you'll be asked to choose a screen name; then asked to choose a password (to prevent other people from using your AOL account); and then you'll see some pointers on exploring AOL.

2 A dialog box opens asking you to confirm some settings about your physical location, and modem and telephone setup. If these settings are correct, click on Yes. (If you're not sure about these settings, ask a knowledgeable family member or friend.) Otherwise, click on No to reset the options as necessary.

Welcome to America Online!

In just a minute you will sign on to America Online and can begin exploring the service! But first, we need to make sure we know how to call America Online from your computer.

America Online will automatically dial a special toll-free "800" number and allow you to choose your access numbers. These numbers will be used for all future connections.

You probably...
- live in the continental United States
- are using America Online at home
- have a 9600 baud (or faster) modem on COM2
- need to dial a "1" to make a toll-free call
- have a touch-tone telephone

If this is all correct, or you're not sure, click "Yes" below. Otherwise, click "No" to adjust America Online to work properly on your computer.

[Yes]   [No]   [Cancel]

3 Read and carefully follow the on-screen directions, clicking on OK or Continue as necessary to move on to the next dialog box or window. After a few dialog boxes, the software will automatically dial a toll-free (1-800) number to help you determine your local AOL *access numbers.* Access numbers are local telephone numbers that AOL for Windows uses to connect to AOL; this saves you the cost of making long-distance telephone calls to Virginia.

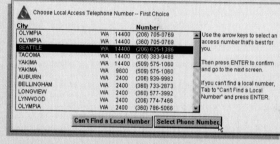

Choose Local Access Telephone Number -- First Choice

City			Number	
OLYMPIA	WA	14400	(206) 705-0769	
OLYMPIA	WA	14400	(360) 705-0769	
SEATTLE	WA	14400	(206) 625-1386	
TACOMA	WA	14400	(206) 383-9488	
YAKIMA	WA	14400	(509) 575-1060	
YAKIMA	WA	9600	(509) 575-1060	
AUBURN	WA	2400	(206) 939-9982	
BELLINGHAM	WA	2400	(360) 733-2873	
LONGVIEW	WA	2400	(360) 577-3992	
LYNWOOD	WA	2400	(206) 774-7466	
OLYMPIA	WA	2400	(360) 786-5066	

Use the arrow keys to select an access number that's best for you.

Then press ENTER to confirm and go to the next screen.

If you can't find a local number, Tab to "Can't Find a Local Number" and press ENTER.

[Can't Find a Local Number]   [Select Phone Numbers]

4 Once AOL for Windows has successfully connected to the toll-free number, you will be asked to provide your local area code. Once you do, you'll be given a list of telephone numbers in or near that area code. Select a local number (one that you can call without incurring a long-distance charge), and then click on Select Phone Number.

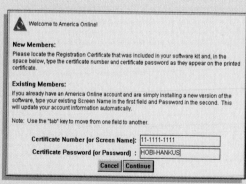

Welcome to America Online!

New Members:
Please locate the Registration Certificate that was included in your software kit and, in the space below, type the certificate number and certificate password as they appear on the printed certificate.

Existing Members:
If you already have an America Online account and are simply installing a new version of the software, type your existing Screen Name in the first field and Password in the second. This will update your account information automatically.

Note: Use the "tab" key to move from one field to another.

Certificate Number (or Screen Name): [11-1111-1111]
Certificate Password (or Password): [HOBI-HANKUS]

[Cancel] [Continue]

5 You'll be asked to select a secondary local access number (as a backup in case your first number is busy) and to confirm your two choices. Then AOL for Windows will disconnect from the toll-free number and call one of your local access numbers. Once connected, you'll be asked to provide the registration number and password that came with your installation disks. Type these in carefully, and then click on Continue. Be sure to use the information included with *your* installation disk(s), *not* the information shown here.

How to Leave and Return to America Online

O nce you've signed on to AOL, the clock starts ticking. Don't panic; you probably have some free time coming to you, and even after using that up, few people spend so much time on AOL that it breaks the family budget. However, prudent use of your online time will save you money in the long run. The most important step in using online time efficiently is to learn how to *sign off* (disconnect) from AOL. Even if you're just getting up to get a drink, go ahead and sign off; it's easy to do and easy to sign back on, and it saves you money. Let's see how to sign off and sign on.

TIP SHEET

► If you inadvertently close the Welcome window, you can reopen it by choosing Set Up & Sign On from the Go To menu.

► If you want to save yourself the trouble of typing your password each time you sign on, you can *store* your password. To do so, choose Set Preferences from the Members menu, click on Passwords, type your password in the text box, and then click on OK. (You can do all of this while you're signed off.) If you store your password, bear in mind that anyone who has access to your computer can then use your AOL account.

► As you explore AOL, your screen can become filled with many windows. Although you can close or minimize these windows (see Chapter 2), don't waste your time with these actions if you're going to sign off anyway. Instead, simply sign off. When you sign back on, the windows will have been closed for you.

► **1** Anytime you're on line, to sign off choose Exit from the File menu. (Or click on the close box.) A dialog box opens to ask if you really want to sign off.

8 If your sign-on is successful, you'll be welcomed back to AOL.

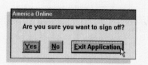

2 If you want to sign off from AOL but keep the AOL for Windows software running, click on Yes. Then skip to step 4. (You'll learn in later chapters some advantages of leaving the software running even after you've signed off.)

3 If you want to sign off from AOL *and* exit AOL for Windows, click on Exit Application. Then skip to step 5.

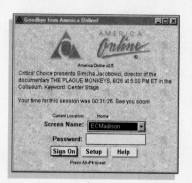

4 If you clicked on Yes, your computer will disconnect from AOL, and the Goodbye from America Online! window will open.

5 If you click on Exit Application, AOL for Windows will close, and you'll be returned to the Desktop. To restart the software, click on the Start button, point to Programs, point to the America Online program group, and click on the America Online program item; a Welcome window will open.

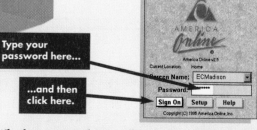

Type your password here...

...and then click here.

6 Whether you see the Goodbye from America Online! or the Welcome window, you sign back on the same way: Type your password in the Password text box (for security reasons, your password will display as asterisks), and then click on Sign On. (To instead close AOL for Windows, choose Exit from the File menu. Version 1.1 users must then click on Yes.)

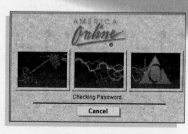

7 AOL for Windows dials one of your local access numbers, makes the connection to America Online, and checks your password.

CHAPTER 4

Exploring America Online

 AOL has so much to offer that it is divided into 14 separate *departments*, from News to Personal Finance to Entertainment. Each department in turn is subdivided into *areas* (also known as *services* or *features*). Even with all this organization, however, it's easy to become overwhelmed by the immense amount of available information.

Relax. Along with its neatly categorized information, AOL and AOL for Windows together provide many tools to help you get around, including the Flashbar, a Directory of Services, and keywords. AOL also has a special area just to find New Features and Services. This chapter shows you how to use these tools. In addition, you'll learn how to keep track of your online time and charges, so that you don't inadvertently break the family budget in your enthusiasm to explore.

So put on your pith helmet and some khaki shorts, fill your canteen, and hold on tight to your mouse and keyboard—you're going exploring!

Note: AOL is immense, and it gets bigger every day as new information and new services are added. Because of the size and constant growth of this online service, no book can possibly cover its every aspect. What this book does, instead, is show you many of AOL's most useful and interesting features, while teaching you about tools that you can use to efficiently explore AOL on your own. So come with us as we explore, but if you get the urge to strike out on your own, go ahead—we promise to wait for you.

How to Use the Flashbar

The Flashbar sits right below the menu bar. It contains icons to help you get around in AOL, as well as to help you send information to and save information from AOL. Many Flashbar icons are shortcuts for commands you would otherwise issue from menus. To use a Flashbar icon, simply click on it. We'll show you many of these icons in use throughout this book.

1 Click on the Read New Mail icon to see a list of any electronic mail that you've received. This is a shortcut for choosing Read New Mail from the Mail menu. To open a form for sending electronic mail to others, click on the Compose Mail icon. This is a shortcut for choosing Compose Mail from the Mail menu. (Chapter 7 shows you how to send and receive electronic mail.)

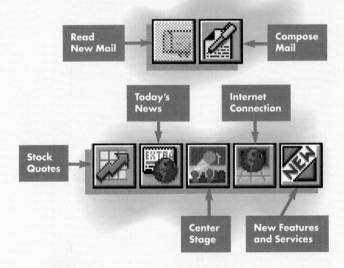

TIP SHEET

▶ Although five Flashbar icons (Compose Mail, Download Manager, Print, Save, and Favorite Places) can often be used offline, the rest are available only for online use. When Flashbar icons are unavailable, they usually appear dimmed.

▶ You *must* use the mouse (or some other pointing device) to access the Flashbar. If you're working without a pointing device, you'll need to use the menu bar instead. For the Flashbar icons with no direct menu equivalent, you can use keywords instead, as described later in this chapter.

▶ Similar to Flashbar icons, the buttons you see in the Welcome! and Main Menu windows when you first sign on can also help you get around AOL.

▶ If you can't remember what feature or service an icon represents, point your mouse to it, and the name of the icon will appear on your screen.

10 Click on Favorite Places as a shortcut to access your favorite AOL places.

9 Click on the Print icon to send the contents of the current document window to your printer. Click on the Save icon to send the contents of the current document window to a hard- or floppy-disk file. The Print and Save icons work only when the current document window contains information suitable for printing or saving.

2 Click on the Main Menu icon to go to the Main menu where AOL's department icons are listed. Click on the Member Services icon as a shortcut to choosing Member Services from the Members menu.

3 Click on the Directory of Services icon as a shortcut for choosing Directory of Services from the Go To menu. (You'll learn how to use the Directory on the next page.) Click on People Connection as a shortcut to choosing Lobby from the Go To Menu.

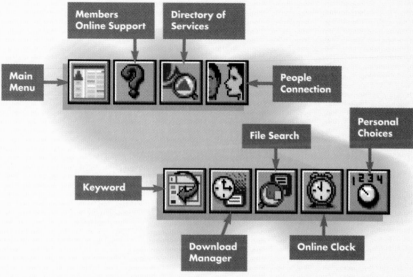

4 Click on the Stock Quotes icon to go to the Quotes & Portfolios area. This icon is a shortcut for choosing the same area in the Go To menu. The Today's News, Center Stage, and Internet Connection icons are other Shortcuts.

5 Click on the New Services icon to go to the New Features & Services area. (As you might expect, this area describes AOL's newest features and services.) The Discover America Online icon is another shortcut.

6 Click on the Keyword icon to open the Go To Keyword window. This is a shortcut for choosing Keyword from the Go To menu. (You'll learn about keywords later in this chapter.)

8 Click on the Online Clock icon to see the current time and how long you've been online during your current AOL session. This is a shortcut for choosing Online Clock from the Go To menu. Personal Choices is another shortcut.

7 Click on the Download Manager icon as a shortcut for choosing Download Manager from the File menu. Click on the File Search icon to open the File Search window. This item is not available on any menu. (Chapter 8 shows you how to search for and download files.)

How to Use the Directory of Services

One of the challenges of using an online service as large and diverse as AOL is finding out what's available. It's like exploring a large, unfamiliar city without a printed tour guide: You can wander around for hours or even days before stumbling upon something that really intrigues you. That's where AOL's *Directory of Services* comes in. Like a well-designed tour guide, the Directory provides a wealth of descriptions that help you quickly and easily identify AOL areas that might interest you. As an added bonus, the Directory can even transport you to any described area.

TIP SHEET

▶ **An active More button (see step 5) is a common sight near AOL list boxes; it indicates that the current list is only a partial list. (Note the line above the list box in step 5—"Items 1–20 of 43 matching entries"—indicating that 23 more list items are available.) Whenever you display a list that exceeds 20 items, AOL generally shows you only the first 20 items, and then activates the More button. Click on that button to add more items to the list—up to 20 at a time. Once every available item is listed, the More button will dim.**

▶ **An area description often lists the area's *location* (see the bottom of the list box in step 6). The location shows how to reach the described area without using a shortcut such as the Directory of Services.**

▶ **The Directory of Services is just one example of AOL's many *searchable databases*. You'll learn more about them in Chapter 11.**

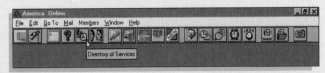

1 Make sure you're signed on to AOL, and then click on the Flashbar's Directory of Services icon. (Or choose Directory of Services from the Go To menu.)

8 You are directly transported to that service.

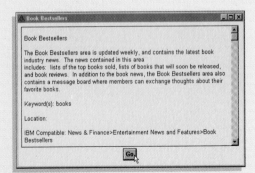

7 To explore the described service further, click on Go.

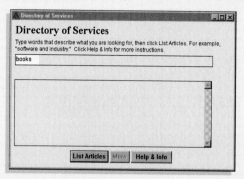

2 A Directory of Services window opens. Double-click on Search the Directory of Services.

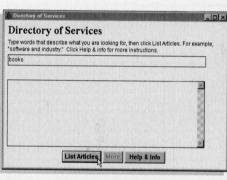

3 A second Directory of Services window opens. In the blank text box at the top of this window, type a *search criterion*. A search criterion is a word or words that indicate the type of service you are seeking. For example, if you want to play a game, you could type **games**; if you're interested in book reviews, you could type **books**.

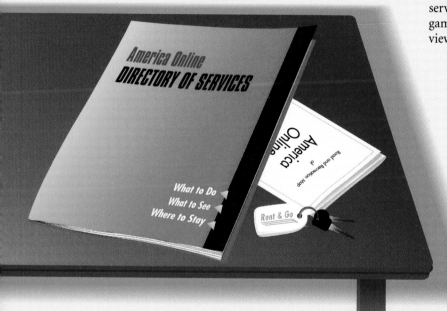

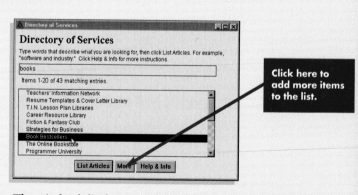

4 Click on List Articles.

Click here to add more items to the list.

5 The window's list box now displays the services related to your search criterion. If you don't see a service that interests you, scroll down through the list. If there are more services available than will fit in the list box, the More button will be available for you to click to list additional services. Once you find a listing that *does* interest you, double-click on it.

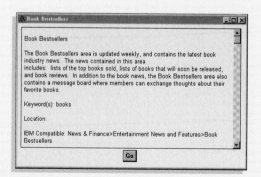

6 A new window opens, containing a description of the service you selected. Use the scroll bar as necessary to read the service's description.

How to Find Out about New Features and Services

Looking for something new to explore or just want to know what's hot this month on AOL? AOL is constantly working to add interesting new features and services so you'll never get bored. Whether it's in an area you're already visiting or an new area you've never tried, next time you need a little something new to spice up your life click on the New Services icon and get ready to explore.

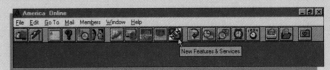

▶ **1** Let's see what's new. Make sure you're signed on to AOL, and then click on the Flashbar's New Services icon. (Or choose New Services from the Go To menu.)

7 The What's Hot This Month window opens. Scroll through the window listing until you find an interesting item and click on Open (or double-click on the item).

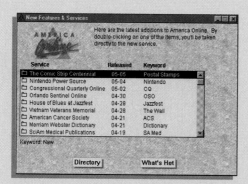

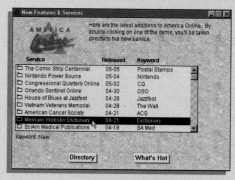

2 The New features and Services window opens showing you the latest editions to AOL in a window's list box. There are also two buttons on this window—Directory and What's Hot. Skip to step 5 to use the Directory button, and What's Hot.

3 Choose one of the items in the list box. If you don't see a service that interests you, scroll down through the list. Once you find an item that does interest you, double-click on it.

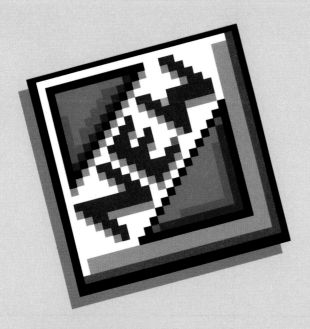

4 A new window opens, containing the feature or service you selected. Now is your chance to explore the new service. When you're ready to try another new feature go back to step 3.

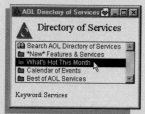

6 The Directory of Services window opens. Choose What's Hot This Month in the window listing and double-click. (What's Hot This Month can also be opened from the New Features & Services window by clicking on the What's Hot button.)

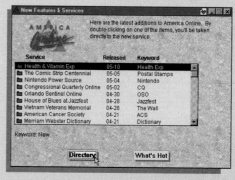

5 Click on the Directory button.

How to Use Keywords

O nce you start getting familiar with AOL and discovering certain departments and areas that you want to visit regularly, you'll come to appreciate keywords. Using a keyword is like taking a taxi: You give the driver an address, and then sit back for the ride. You don't have to know the route because the driver takes care of that for you. New in town and don't know any addresses? No problem—just like a friendly and knowledgeable taxi driver, AOL will provide some address suggestions for you.

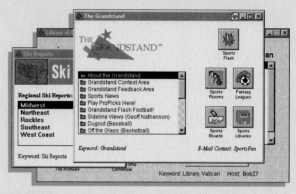

▶ **1** When you visit an area that you want to come back to, look for the area's keyword. Keywords are usually displayed near the bottom of the area's window. Make a mental note of the keyword, or jot it down. (If you haven't explored enough yet to find a suitable keyword, don't worry; we'll help you out on that in a moment.)

TIP SHEET

▶ **You will find keywords mentioned all over AOL, inviting you to jump from one place to another. If you're intrigued, give in to the urge. When it's time to return to your original window, simply close or minimize any new windows you've opened. Or, try returning to a previous window by choosing its name from the Window taskbar.**

▶ **Good keywords are like gold. Once you find a keyword that works for you, hold on to it; not every area displays a keyword, even if one exists.**

▶ **If you find that you use certain keywords frequently, or if you just have trouble remembering your favorite keywords, try adding them to the Go To menu. To do this, choose Edit Go To Menu from the Go To menu.**

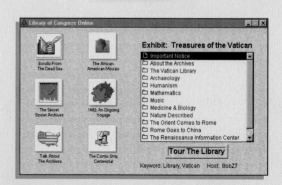

8 You are directly transported to the department or area specified by your keyword.

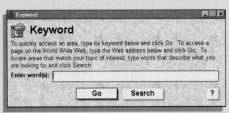

2 Let's see how to use a keyword. Make sure you're signed on to AOL, and then click on the Flashbar's Keyword icon. (Or choose Keyword from the Go To menu.)

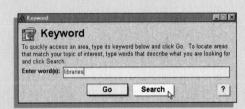

3 The Go To Keyword window opens. If you know which keyword you want to use, skip now to step 7. Otherwise, continue on to step 4.

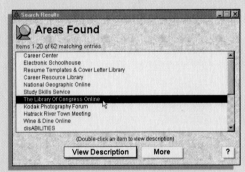

4 If you don't know which keyword you need, enter the topic you're interested in and click Search.

5 Select an item from the window listing (you may need to scroll) and click View Description to find out more about this topic.

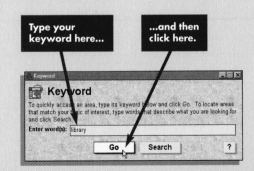

6 To go to the keyword area for this item, click GO (you may want to note the keyword at the end of the description for future use). Skip to Step 8.

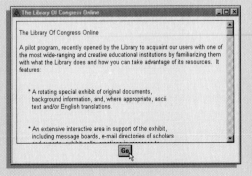

7 Type your keyword in the Enter Keyword text box, and then click on GO. Note that keywords are not *case sensitive*; that is, it doesn't matter if you type a keyword in all uppercase (*LIBRARY*), lowercase (*library*), or some mixture of the two (*LiBrArY*). You'll still end up in the same place.

How to Keep Track of Your Online Time and Charges

After using up any free or credited minutes you might have, every extra minute you spend on AOL costs money. It's not a tremendous amount of money, but it's still a good idea to keep track of your online time and charges so that things don't get out of hand. An unexpectedly large online service bill is bad for you (because you have to pay it), as well as for AOL (because then they have an unhappy customer). To help prevent such a problem, AOL makes it easy for you to see how long you've been on line during your current session. Or if you want to see your overall charges for the current billing cycle, AOL can show you that, too.

▶ **1** To see how long you've been online during your current session, click on the Flashbar's Online Clock icon. (Or, choose Online Clock from the Go To menu.)

TIP SHEET

▶ **Billing terms**—such as how many minutes you're credited when you first join AOL, your monthly membership fee, how many free minutes are included in that fee, and so on—might differ among members and across time. To see the exact billing terms of *your* membership, repeat steps 3 and 4, click on Explain Billing Terms, and then click on Open.

▶ Your current month's billing summary reflects all of your chargeable online time, *except* for the current online session. For the most accurate summary, sign off and back on again, and then look at the summary immediately.

▶ *Free minutes* are the minutes you get every month as part of your monthly membership fee. *Credited minutes* are additional minutes that you might receive, for example, as a gift for joining AOL or as compensation for some online difficulty you've had.

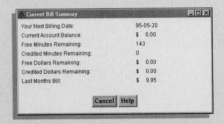

6 A Current Bill Summary window opens, showing you your next billing date; your current balance for online charges (exclusive of your monthly membership fee); how many free and credited minutes (if any) you have remaining for this cycle; your remaining free and credited dollars (if any); and last month's overall service bill (including your monthly membership fee).

2 A dialog box opens, showing you the current time and how long you've been on line. Click on OK to close the dialog box.

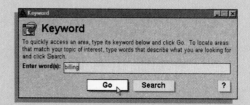

3 To see all of your charges for the current monthly billing cycle, use the keyword **billing**.

5 A Billing Information and Changes window opens, listing a variety of options. Click on Current Month's Billing Summary, and then click on Open. (Or simply double-click on Current Month's Billing Summary.)

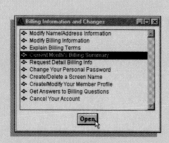

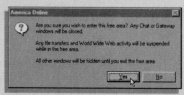

4 A dialog box opens, indicating that you are about to enter a free area. (Free areas are discussed in Chapter 5.) Click on Yes.

TRY IT!

Here's a hands-on opportunity to practice some of the techniques involved in using Directory of Services, Keyword searches, and checking the Online Clock. In this exercise, you'll use many of the techniques you've read about in Chapter 4, as well as some important techniques from earlier chapters. Chapter numbers are included in parentheses at the end of each step to show you where we first introduced the technique required to perform that step. (**Note:** Before attempting this activity, be sure that you have installed AOL for Windows and have set up your AOL membership account. For details, see Chapter 3.)

1

If necessary, turn on your computer.

2

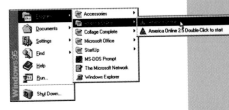

Start America Online for Windows. From your Windows Desktop click Start, point to Programs, then point to the America Online program group and click on the America Online item (*Chapter 3*).

Ready when you are!

3

Verify that your screen name (not the one shown here) is displayed in the Screen Name drop-down list box, and then type your password in the Password text box (*Chapter 3*).

4

Click on Sign On (*Chapter 3*).

5

Wait a few moments as AOL for Windows dials your local access number, connects to AOL, checks your password and then opens the online Welcome! window (*Chapter 3*).

6

Click on the Flashbar's Directory of Services icon (*Chapter 4*).

7

Type **games** in the search criterion box (*Chapter 4*).

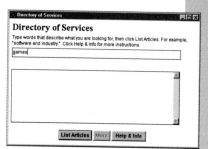

8

Click on List Articles (*Chapter 4*).

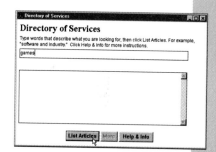

9

In the windows list box double click on Cartoons (*Chapter 4*).

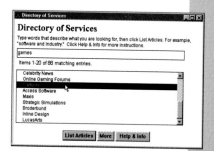

Continue to next page ▶

TRY IT!

Continue
below

12

Click on the
Flashbar's Keyword icon (*Chapter 4*).

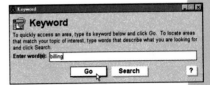

13

Type **billing**
in the Enter
words text
box, and then click Go (*Chapter 4*).

10

In the
Cartoons
windows list
box select
Dilbert
Comics and
click on open
(*Chapter 4*).

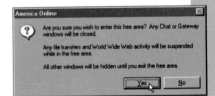

14

Click on Yes
(*Chapter 4*).

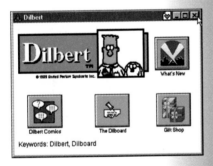

11

Close the
open win-
dows by
clicking the
Windows
Close button
in the upper-
right corner
(*Chapter 2*).

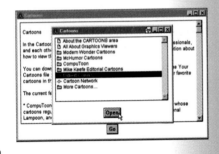

15

Choose
Current
Month's
Billing
Summary
and then
click on
Open
(*Chapter 4*).

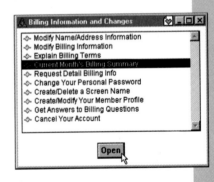

16

Click on
Cancel to
close this
window
(*Chapter 4*).

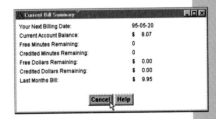

Click on the
Flashbar's Online Clock icon
(*Chapter 4*).

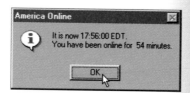

Click OK to
close this
window
(*Chapter 4*).

Choose Exit
from the File
menu
(*Chapter 3*).

Click on Exit
Application
to both sign
off from AOL and exit AOL for
Windows (*Chapter 3*).

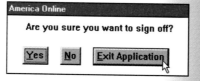

CHAPTER 5

Help!

Confused? Lost? Just plain stuck?

Relax. No matter how many books you read or how much computer experience you have, you're bound to need some help with AOL now and then. Knowing this, AOL provides easily accessible help in two forms: *online help* and *offline help.*

Online help is stored on AOL's computers in Virginia, and there's plenty of it. You can get up-to-date, ready-to-use help for just about any AOL question you have. For example, you can find out how to make AOL for Windows run better on your computer, how to determine an Internet address, how to find a specific area within AOL, or how to locate online job listings. As an added bonus, you can do all this for free because using online help incurs *no online charges!*

Unfortunately, online help has no value if what you need is help to get online in the first place. That's where offline help comes in handy. Offline help is stored on your own computer's hard drive, so it's accessible whether or not you're signed on to AOL. Like online help, offline help is also free to use—that is, as long as you use it off line.

This chapter introduces you to the wonderful worlds of offline and online help.

How to Get Offline Help

Why won't my new modem dial when I click on Sign On? How can I connect to AOL when I'm away from home? How can I change my local access numbers? Can I get my modem to stop making those annoying sounds when I first sign on? The answers to these and many more questions are waiting for you in offline help.

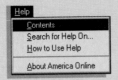

 TIP SHEET

▶ Another convenient way to get offline help is to *search* for help much as you would search a searchable database (see Chapter 11). To start searching for help, choose Search for Help On, in the AOL for Windows Help menu.

▶ To get offline help on using offline help, choose How to Use Help from any Help menu.

▶ If you can't find the help you need in offline help, and you aren't able to sign on to AOL, you still have at least two other options: You can call AOL by telephone at 1-800-827-6364, or you can use another communications program (such as Windows HyperTerminal) to call AOL's Technical Support BBS (bulletin board system) by modem at 1-800-827-5808.

▶ When using offline help, bear in mind that some of the information may be out of date. For the most current information, double-check with online help, if possible (see next page).

▶ **1** Start AOL for Windows, but don't sign on to AOL. (If you *can* sign on, you might as well skip right to the next page to learn about online help.) Then choose Contents from the Help menu.

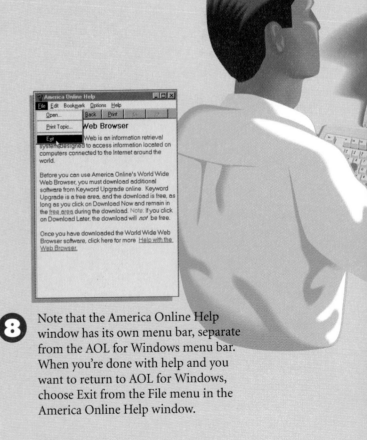

8 Note that the America Online Help window has its own menu bar, separate from the AOL for Windows menu bar. When you're done with help and you want to return to AOL for Windows, choose Exit from the File menu in the America Online Help window.

 Continue clicking, scrolling, and reading until you have the information you need.

2 The America Online Help application window opens, listing available help topics. (Your Help window may look different from this one.)

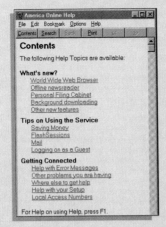

3 Every help topic has a solid underline. Scroll to find an appropriate topic, and then click on it.

4 A new help screen appears, displaying information on your selected topic. Scroll to read the topic. If this help screen, too, displays solid-underlined topics, click on those topics as desired to jump to other help screens.

5 To return to a previous help screen, click on Back.

6 Sometimes you'll come across a word or phrase with a dotted underline. To see a definition of that word or phrase, click on it; a box containing the definition opens. Once you've read the definition, click on the box to close it.

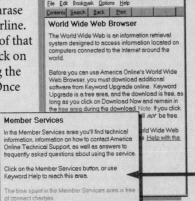

How to Get Online Help

Like offline help, AOL's online help provides screen after screen of useful solutions. Online help, though, takes help one step further. You see, if you have a problem or question for which AOL has no ready answer, you still have *three* additional online methods for finding a solution: by chatting live with AOL's Customer Service technicians, by sending an e-mail to Customer Relations, or by presenting your problem to fellow AOL members through a message board. Between all the prepared solutions and these three live resources, you'll be able to solve just about any AOL problem.

▶ **1** Make sure you're signed on to AOL, then click on the Flashbar's Member Services icon. (Or choose Member Services from the members menu.)

8 Once you've found your solution, or at least left a message asking for one, choose Exit Free Area from the Go To menu. A dialog box informs you that your online time charges will resume. Click on Yes to continue; any windows that were hidden when you entered the free area will reappear.

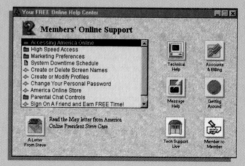

7 If you can't find the answer you need, return to Your FREE Online Help Center, and then click on either Tech Live Support or Member to Member. Tech Live Support enables you to chat with AOL's Customer Service technicians. Member to Member enables you to send an e-mail to AOL's Customer Relations department or takes you to a message board dedicated to problem solving among AOL members.

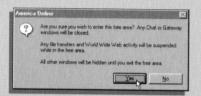

2 A dialog box informs you that you're about to enter a free area. This dialog box also warns that certain windows will be closed, or temporarily hidden, until you leave the free area. Click on Yes to continue.

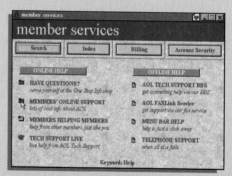

3 Next, you'll see Free Help Area. As soon as this window appears, you can take a moment and relax, knowing that you're no longer being charged for your online time. Then, click on Members Online Support.

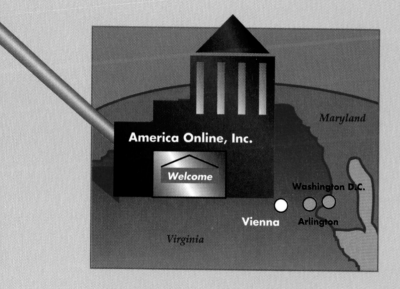

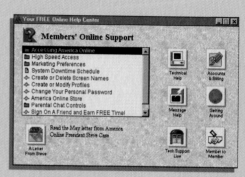

4 Scroll through the list box to see if anything there can help you with your problem. If you find something, double-click on it and continue from there. Otherwise, continue on to step 5.

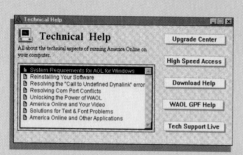

6 All the buttons mentioned in step 5 take you to a specialized help window such as this one. From here, double-click on list-box items and/or click on buttons until you arrive at a window that displays the prepared solution you need.

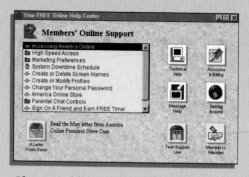

5 If your problem is related to running AOL for Windows on your computer, click on the Technical Help button. If you have a question about online charges or if you want to change your account information, click on Accounts & Billing. For help with using message boards, e-mail, or chat rooms, click on Message Help. To find out about various AOL services, click on Getting Around.

CHAPTER 6

Using Message Boards

AOL is an electronic *community* comprising AOL's many members. It provides a collection of electronic information both produced by AOL and contributed from its members. AOL members' contributions add to the richness of AOL's features by providing an intriguing personal side to information. In this chapter, Chapter 7, and Chapter 10, we'll show you ways to interact with other AOL members, through message boards, electronic mail, and chat rooms.

This chapter introduces *message boards*—sometimes known as *bulletin boards.* Like the cork-and-pushpin message boards you see in many grocery stores, libraries, and laundromats, AOL's electronic message boards offer places for people to openly post messages (often called *postings*) for other people to read. In most cases, messages are exchanged primarily among members, but some boards do specialize in exchanging messages between members and AOL employees or vendors.

Unlike those grocery-store boards, though, AOL's message boards don't usually contain many one-way messages such as "Bake Sale This Friday." Rather, these electronic boards promote lively, multiple-member discussions and debates on subjects ranging from politics to health to fine dining. In this way, AOL's electronic message boards are more like community meetings. Read on to learn more.

How to Peruse a Message Board

To prevent message-board chaos, AOL provides dozens of subject-specific boards. This way, members interested primarily in politics, for instance, don't have to wade through dozens of messages on health. Message boards are scattered all over AOL, so you're bound to stumble across one eventually. When you do find a board that interests you—a likely occurrence, as you'll be exploring areas that interest you, anyway—your first logical step is to peruse the board to see what kind of discussions and debates are there. This page shows you how to get to know a message board on your first visit.

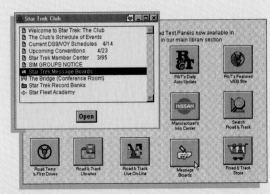

1 As you explore AOL, keep your eye out for buttons or list-box items that lead to message boards. Generally, these buttons and items display pushpin icons and/or include the words *message* and/or *board*. To access a board using a button, click on the button; to access a message using a list-box item, double-click on the item.

8 To read the messages in another topic, return to the topics window and repeat steps 5 through 7. To read messages in another category, return to the subjects window, and repeat steps 4 through 7.

The Next Generation/USS-Enterprise

Subj: Re:Galaxy Class
Date: 95-01-25 02:27:51 EDT
From: DavidC8169

First, the Enterprise in AGT was not real, the whole episode was a fantasy created by Q to teach Picard a lesson.

Second, according to the Tech Manual Starfleet only built six Galaxy class ships. The Odyssey, Enterprise, Galaxy, Yamato and two more unnamed vessels. Odyssey was destroyed by the Jem Hadar, Yamato was destroyed by a computer virus, the Galaxy is still

Previous Message   Add Message   Next Message

7 When you're done reading the current message, click on Next Message to display the next message in your selected topic. (You can also review earlier messages by clicking on Previous Message.) Repeat this step as desired to read the remaining messages. Once you've read every message in the current topic, the Next Message button dims.

TIP SHEET

► If you're unsure of a board's specific purpose or how to access a unique board feature, try clicking on the Help & Info button in the board's initial window. (If this button is unavailable, see Chapter 5 for information on other sources of help.)

► To see a list of messages contained within a topic instead of jumping right to the first message, in step 5 click on the List Messages button rather than on Read Message.

► After you've visited a board once, or if there are too many messages for you to read in one session, try taking advantage of the Find New and Find Since buttons (available in most boards). Find New lists only messages that have been posted since your last visit to this board; Find Since lists only messages that have been posted since a date that you specify.

2 Like online magazines (see Chapter 13), every message board is different. Typically, though, message boards use electronic *folders* (similar in function to the manila folders used in a filing cabinet) to divide and organize messages into separate topics. Popular message boards, like the one shown here, first divide messages into categories, which are in turn divided into topic folders.

3 The initial window for a typical message board provides a set of buttons for perusing the board. If your board is divided first into categories (like the board shown here), the window generally will display a List Categories button. If it does, click on that button and then move on to step 4. If your board is divided into topics only, there will generally be a Browse Folders button; if so, click on that button and then skip to step 5.

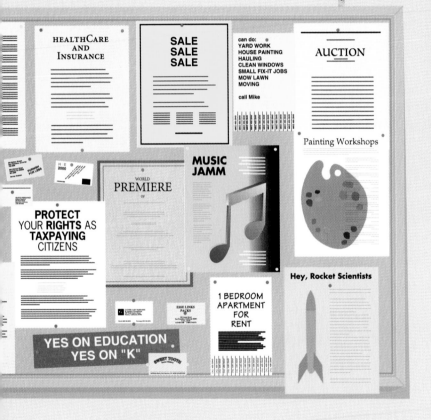

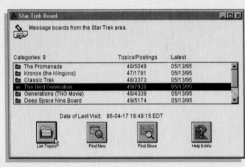

4 A new window opens, listing available categories. Scroll to find a category that interests you, click on that category, and then click on List Topics. (Or simply double-click on the category.)

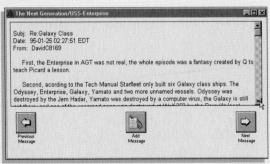

6 The first message in the selected topic opens. Scroll to read the message.

5 A new window opens, listing available topics. Scroll to find a topic that interests you, click on that topic, and then click on Read 1st Message.

How to Post a Message

Now you know how to peruse a message board. Just perusing the board, however, is akin to listening in on a conversation but never speaking your mind. To take an *active* part in the conversation, you need to post your own messages. As with face-to-face conversations, your online messages can express opinions and insights, ask questions, give responses, or whatever—just as long as the messages are fairly meaningful and related to the topic at hand. Posting messages on a regular basis keeps your favorite message board lively and interesting for all participants and makes you an active "citizen" of the AOL community. After all, what good is a message board with no messages?

TIP SHEET

▸ **You have virtually unlimited space when typing a message. Keep in mind, however, that very few readers have the interest or inclination to read l-o-n-n-n-g messages.**

▸ **Remember that your message may be read by hundreds or even thousands of people from varying backgrounds, so be careful what you write and how you write it. In general, avoid profanity, snide and discriminatory remarks, and personal attacks. Watch out for subtle jokes, too— without the help of body language usually present in face-to-face conversations, your message may appear to be offensive, even if you didn't intend it to be.**

▸ **If you can't find an appropriate existing topic for your message, try creating a new topic folder and posting your message there. To create a topic folder, list the topics most closely related to your new topic, and then click on Create Topic.**

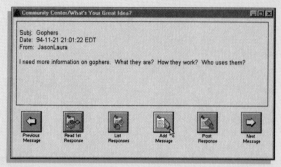

1 To respond to a specific message, open the message and then click on Add Message. For a more general message—one that isn't in direct response to another message—you can instead list the messages within an appropriate topic, and then click on Post Message. (To see how to list topic messages, see the second Tip on the previous page.)

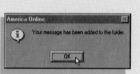

7 If all is well, a dialog box opens telling you that your message has been added to the current topic folder. Click on OK to close the dialog box.

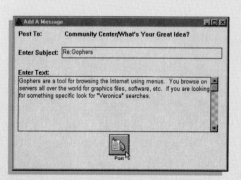
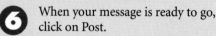

6 When your message is ready to go, click on Post.

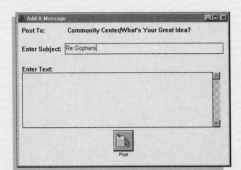

2 Whichever button you click on, the Add A Message window opens. This is where you identify your message subject and write the body of your message.

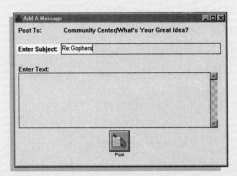

3 If you clicked on Add Message in step 1, then the Enter Subject text box already reflects the subject of the message to which you're responding. In general, you can leave this text as is; that makes it easier for other readers to follow the various conversations within a topic. If you instead clicked on Post Message in step 1, the Enter Subject text box will be empty; in that case, type some appropriate text here.

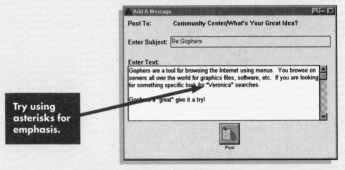

Try using asterisks for emphasis.

4 Click in the Enter Text text box, and type your message. Avoid using all uppercase characters; IT'S LIKE SHOUTING! To add emphasis to a particular word or phrase without using upper-case, enclose that word or phrase within some *attention-getting* punctuation, such as the asterisks shown here.

5 Once you've finished typing, use your arrow keys, Delete, and Backspace as necessary to review and edit your message thoroughly. Remember, once you post your message, there's no taking it back; this is your last chance to make sure that you're saying exactly what you mean to say.

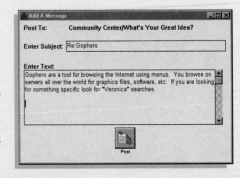

CHAPTER 7

Sending and Receiving Electronic Mail

In Chapter 6, you learned how to communicate with other AOL members through message boards. Although message boards are an excellent way to share your thoughts with dozens or even hundreds of other people, they aren't very private. And as bold and outspoken as you might be, there are some matters that are just too personal or too confidential to share with a large group of unknown readers.

When you want to send private messages, try AOL's Mail feature. Like its paper counterpart, electronic mail (also known as *e-mail*) is designed for more private communications—but without the waste of paper, envelopes, and stamps. Besides the privacy factor, AOL's e-mail system has many other advantages over message boards: For instance, you don't have to depend on your recipients checking the appropriate board, because the moment they sign on, they are automatically notified of any new e-mail they've received. You can send AOL messages to many other e-mail systems (the Internet, CompuServe, MCI Mail, and so on), too. And if your recipient isn't connected to *any* e-mail system, you can use AOL's Mail to send a fax or even an old-fashioned stamp-and-envelope letter. All of these benefits, along with its ease of use, makes Mail one of AOL's most popular features.

And the U.S. Postal Service thinks self-adhesive stamps are *progress*?

How to Send Mail to Other AOL Members

Composing and sending e-mail to other AOL members is easy. You type up a message just as you would to send it by traditional mail, but instead of going through the bother of printing the message, addressing and stamping an envelope, and running down to the corner mailbox, you just click on a few on-screen buttons. AOL e-mail is inexpensive, too. Unlike some other online services, AOL lets you send as many mail messages as you want at no extra charge. As an added bonus, you can even save yourself some online charges by composing your mail messages off line; when you're ready, you only have to sign on for the few seconds it takes to send your mail.

TIP SHEET

▶ If you're unsure of a recipient's screen name, try finding it in AOL's Member Directory. Sign on, choose Members Directory from the Members menu, then choose Search the Member Directory from the list box. (This directory is a searchable database; Chapter 11 describes searchable databases.) If all else fails, call your friend by (gasp!) telephone and ask for the name.

▶ To send multiple mail messages, perform steps 1 through 5 for each message, sign on, and then perform steps 7 and 8 for each message.

▶ To address the same message to more than one member, type all the screen names in the To list box, separating them with commas. Use this same technique in the CC list box to send multiple courtesy copies.

▶ To review, check on the status of, or even *unsend* (retrieve) mail messages that your recipients haven't yet read, sign on, and then choose Check Mail You've Sent from the Mail menu.

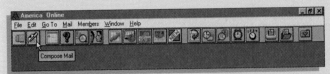

1 Start AOL for Windows, but don't sign on to AOL yet. If you're already signed on, sign off without leaving AOL for Windows. (Refer back to Chapter 3 for details.) Then click on the Flashbar's Compose Mail icon. (Or choose Compose Mail from the Mail menu.)

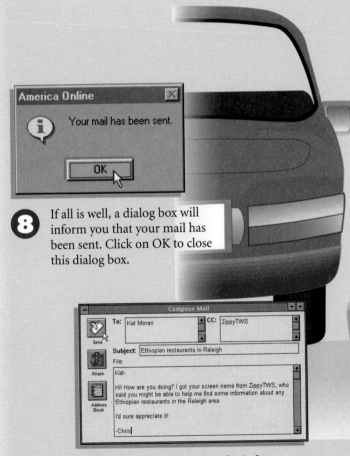

8 If all is well, a dialog box will inform you that your mail has been sent. Click on OK to close this dialog box.

7 In the Compose Mail window, click on Send.

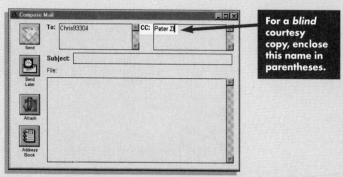

For a *blind* courtesy copy, enclose this name in parentheses.

2 A Compose Mail window opens. In the To list box, type your addressee's screen name.

3 If you want to send a courtesy copy of your message to a second AOL member, type that member's screen name in the CC list box. (To send a *blind* courtesy copy—one that your addressee cannot tell you sent—enclose the screen name in parentheses.)

4 In the Subject text box, type a subject for your message. This is the text your recipients will see before opening your message.

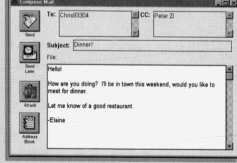

After signing on, move this window out of the way.

5 In the large box at the bottom of the window, type your message. As with message-board messages, you have virtually unlimited typing space, but try to be as concise as possible. Use your arrow keys, Backspace, and Delete as necessary to review and edit your message.

6 Move the Welcome or Goodbye from America Online! window so that it's in front of the Compose Mail window. (Either choose the window name from the Window menu, or select Set Up & Sign On in the Go To menu.) Sign on to AOL, and then minimize the online Welcome! window to get it out of the way.

How to Read Mail You've Received

One of the nicest things about *sending* mail is that it greatly increases your chances of *receiving* mail in return. If you've been an AOL member for more than a day or so, you may already have received a mail message from AOL President Steve Case, welcoming you to the service. If you've successfully read this message, then you already know the basics of receiving mail; read this page to learn a little more. If, on the other hand, your mail has been piling up because you weren't quite sure how to look at it, then these pages will help you out.

1 You can read new mail, and you can review mail you've already read. To read new mail, continue on to step 2. To review old mail, skip to step 7.

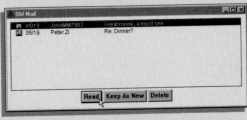

8 The Old Mail window opens, listing all the mail messages you've recently read. (Already-read messages are usually deleted three to five days after they were originally sent.) Click on the message you want to review, and then click on Read. The message will open in its own window, as shown in step 5.

7 To review old mail, make sure you're signed on to AOL, and then choose Check Mail You've Read from the Mail menu.

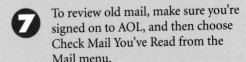

TIP SHEET

▶ **The Welcome! window that opens when you first sign on also contains a button for reading new mail. You can use this button instead of doing step 3 to open the New Mail window.**

▶ **Unread mail usually is deleted 35 days after it was originally sent. To avoid losing unread mail, check your mail at least once every 35 days.**

▶ **If you receive a mail message that you know you'd rather not read, click on that message in the New Mail window, and then click on Ignore. Clicking on Ignore marks the message as read. (If you decide to read it later, you can retrieve it by choosing Check Mail You've Read from the Mail menu.)**

▶ **The Keep As New buttons in the New Mail and Old Mail windows enable you to mark a read or ignored message as unread.**

2 Whenever you're online, look at the Flashbar's Read New Mail icon. If the red flag is up, you've got new mail waiting for you. If the red flag is down, then you have no new mail; you'll either have to wait for someone to send you some mail, or send some mail to yourself just for testing purposes.

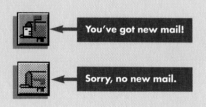

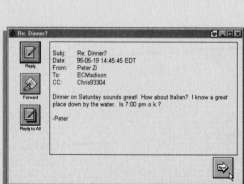

New Mail

Old Mail

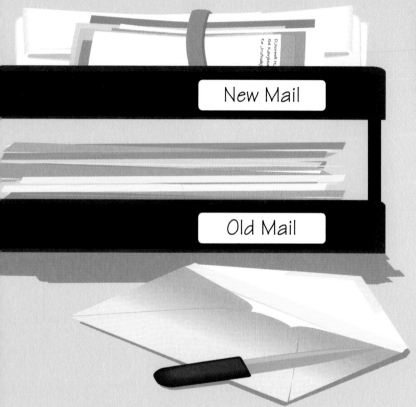

3 If the red flag *is* up, click on the Read New Mail icon. (Or choose Read New Mail from the Mail menu.)

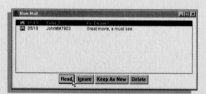

4 A New Mail window opens, listing all the mail messages you've received but haven't yet read. Click on Read.

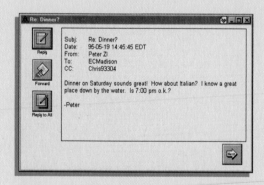

5 The first mail message opens in its own window. Scroll as necessary to read the message. (To keep a permanent copy of the message, you can also save or print it.)

6 If you have more than one mail message waiting, a Next button will appear in the bottom of the message window. Click on this button to display the next message, and then repeat this step as necessary to read all of your mail. Then, you can skip the rest of this activity, or continue on to review old mail.

How to Store Mail on Your Disk

As you use mail more and more you'll no doubt find the need to refer back to a message you've sent or received. Since AOL regularly removes the mail you've read, take advantage of AOL's option to save mail on your computer's hard disk. Messages will then be stored as files on your computer so you can open and re-read your mail anytime, and it's offline so you can save yourself online charges.

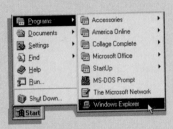

 1 First you'll need to set up a location on your computer's disk to store mail. Open Windows Explorer. From your Windows Desktop click Start, point to Programs, and then click on the Windows Explorer program item.

8 A Save Text As dialog box opens. Use the Drives and Directories boxes as necessary to identify where the message file will be stored on your computer. Type the message's file name (Peter, in this example) in the file name box and click OK.

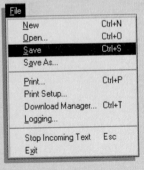

▸ **You can also store mail on your disk that is listed under Check Mail You've Sent or Check Mail You've Received in the Mail menu.**

▸ **Create multiple folders under your C:\AOL25\Mail directory to separate mail you've received from mail you've sent. You can also create subfolders of mail sent or received to sort your mail by subject or perhaps by friends' names.**

 7 To save this message choose Save from the File menu.

2 An Exploring window opens. Find the AOL25 folder, open it by double-clicking on the folder.

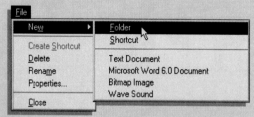

3 To create a new folder under AOL, open the File menu, point to New, and then click on Folder.

4 To name the new folder, type **Mail** in the box next to the folder and press return.

5 Sign on to AOL, then click on the Flashbar's Read New Mail icon. (Or choose Read New Mail from the Mail menu.)

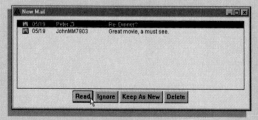

6 Click Read in the New Mail window to open a message.

How to Attach a File to Mail

You probably use programs other than AOL for Windows, such as a word processor (Word, WordPerfect, Ami Pro) or a spreadsheet program (Excel, 1-2-3, Quattro Pro). So you may already know that those programs use disk files to store information in fairly complex formats. AOL's mail messages, however, are only capable of handling a very simple format: plain text. Rather than trying to translate a complex disk file into plain text—thus losing its special formatting and formulas—you can instead *attach* the file to a mail message. When you send your message, the file is copied as is to AOL's computers. When your addressee receives that message, it's a fairly simple task to then copy the file from AOL to his or her own computer.

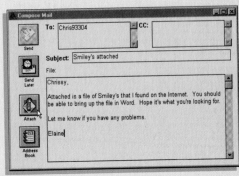

▶ **1** Start composing a mail message as you normally would. (For details, refer back to "How to Send Mail to Another AOL Member" earlier in this chapter.) In the message, explain the purpose of the file that you'll be attaching. Then click on Attach.

TIP SHEET

▶ You have probably heard the terms *uploading* and *downloading*. These words describe the two directions of file transfers. Uploading is the process of transferring files from your computer to another computer. Downloading is the process of transferring files from another computer to your computer. For more information on downloading files from AOL, see Chapter 8.

▶ Although you can use one mail message to send the same file to multiple addressees, you can only attach one file to any one message.

▶ Before sending a file, make sure your addressee has the software necessary to use that file.

▶ It's illegal to send anyone copyrighted files, such as program files, without the express permission to do so.

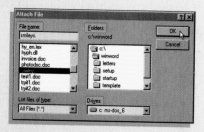

2 An Attach File dialog box opens. Use the Drives and Directories boxes as necessary to identify where the file is stored on your computer. Click on the file in the File Name list box, and then click on OK. (If you need help with drives and directories, consult your Windows documentation.)

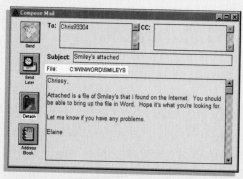

3 When the Attach File dialog box closes, notice that two things have changed in the Compose Mail window: The location and name of your attached file now appear next to the "File:" field above the window's central list box, and the Attach button becomes a Detach button. (As you might expect, the Detach button enables you to remove the current file attachment.)

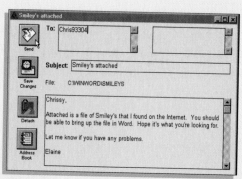

4 If you're already online, click on Send. If not, sign on to AOL, minimize the Welcome! window, and then click on Send.

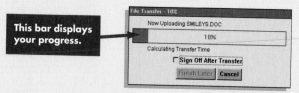

This bar displays your progress.

5 A File Transfer dialog box opens to display the progress of the file transfer from your computer to AOL. The length of this transfer will depend primarily on the file's size and your modem's *baud rate*. (Check your modem's documentation for information on your modem's baud rate.)

6 Once the file transfer is complete, another File Transfer dialog box will open to inform you of that fact. Click on the OK button to close this dialog box.

How to Read an Attached File

Trading files created with special programs—like a word processor or spreadsheet—is easy with AOL's e-mail. Now when you'd like to have someone check over those fine details of your spreadsheet or memo, send them via e-mail.

Since these files contain special formatting, such as underlines, bold characters, or formulas, they must be sent via AOL's e-mail using the Attach feature. When users receive attached files, the files are not readable online since they can only be viewed in the same special program that was used to create them.

AOL has also made unattaching and downloading these files easy for the addressee. No more mailing file disks and waiting days for it to get to its destination; AOL can do it in just minutes.

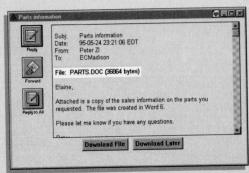

1 Open your mail messages as you normally would. (For details, refer back to "How to Read Mail You've Received" earlier in this chapter.) When you open a message that has a file attached, the message will list the file name and its size.

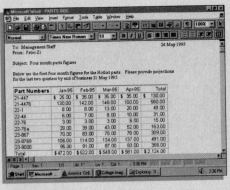

7 The file will open in the program with which it was created.

2 To begin transferring the attached file from AOL to your computer, click on the Download File button.

3 Using the Drives and Directories windows identify a location for the file and click on OK.

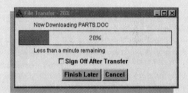

4 A File Transfer dialog box opens to display the progress of your file transfer and the approximate time remaining until the transfer is complete.

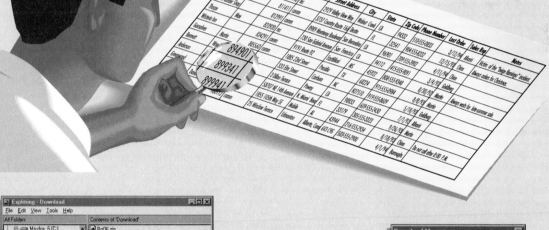

5 Once the file transfer is complete, a Download Manager dialog box will open to inform you of that fact. Click on the OK button to close this dialog box.

6 To view the file that you have transferred, open the Windows Explorer. Click on the Windows Desktop Start button, point to Programs, and then click on Windows Explorer. (For more information please check your Windows Documentation.) Open the appropriate folders (directories) to locate your file, then double-click on the file name to open it.

How to Send Mail Outside of AOL

As you learned at the opening of this chapter, AOL mail isn't limited to mail among AOL members; you also have three options for sending mail to destinations *outside* of AOL. You can send messages to other e-mail systems as *Internet mail*, you can send messages to most U.S. or Canadian fax machines as *fax mail*, and you can even have messages sent via the U.S. Postal Service to any U.S. or Canadian postal address as *paper mail*. The key difference between sending mail to other AOL members and to people outside of AOL is how you address that mail. This page explains the basics of addressing and sending all three types of outside mail.

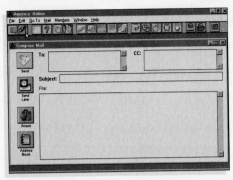

1 Open a Compose Mail window as you normally would to start composing a mail message. (For details, refer back to "How to Send Mail to Other AOL Members" earlier in this chapter.) To send your message as Internet mail, continue on to step 2. To send your message as fax mail, skip to step 4. To send your message as paper mail, skip to step 6.

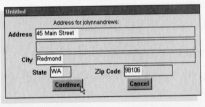

8 A U.S. Mail Return Address dialog box opens, providing text boxes for your return address. Fill in these boxes as appropriate, and then click on Continue. Another dialog box opens, providing text boxes for your recipient's address. Fill in these boxes as appropriate, and then click on Continue again. A third dialog box then opens to inform you that your paper mail has been sent. (At least, it *will* be, within 24 hours.) Click on OK to close this third dialog box.

7 Unlike sending purely electronic mail, paper mail incurs an extra charge that will be billed to your AOL account. A dialog box opens to inform you of the charge. If this is acceptable, click on Yes.

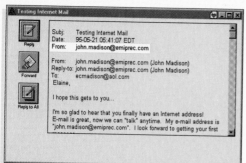

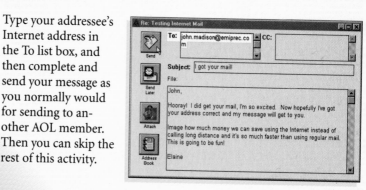

3 Type your addressee's Internet address in the To list box, and then complete and send your message as you normally would for sending to another AOL member. Then you can skip the rest of this activity.

2 Anyone whose e-mail system is connected to the Internet has a unique *Internet address*; it's similar to an AOL screen name. To determine a person's Internet address, ask for it. Or try having that person send you a message first, and then examine that message's From line to determine the return address.

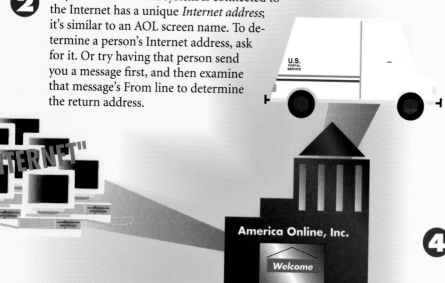

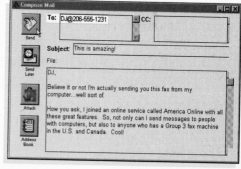

4 To address your message as fax mail, type your addressee's name in the To list box, followed by @ and then the fax area code and telephone number. The addressee name (before the @) can be up to 20 characters long, including letters, numbers, and any punctuation marks except commas and parentheses. Then complete your message, sign on to AOL and bring the Compose Mail window to the front (if necessary), and click on Send.

5 Unlike sending purely electronic mail, fax mail incurs an extra charge that will be billed to your AOL account. A dialog box opens to inform you of the charge. If this is acceptable, click on Yes. A second dialog box then opens to inform you that your fax mail has been sent. (At least, it *will* be, within the hour.) Click on OK to close the second dialog box, and then skip the rest of this activity.

6 To address your message as paper mail, type your addressee's name in the To list box, followed by *@usmail*. The addressee name (before the @) can be up to 33 characters long, including letters, numbers, and any punctuation marks except commas and parentheses. Then complete your message, sign on to AOL and bring the Compose Mail window to the front (if necessary), and click on Send.

How to Use the Address Book

Like postal addresses, *e-mail addresses* (AOL screen names, Internet addresses, and so on) can be difficult to remember. You could maintain a *paper* list of e-mail addresses as you would for postal addresses; a better option, though, is to take advantage of the AOL for Windows Address Book. The Address Book enables you to maintain an *electronic* list of your online correspondent's real names and e-mail addresses. In addition, the Address Book can help you easily and accurately address your mail messages.

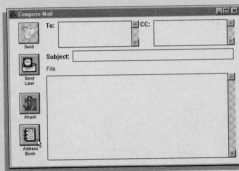

1 Open a Compose Mail window as you normally would to start composing a mail message. (For details, refer back to "How to Send Mail to Other AOL Members" earlier in this chapter.) Rather than typing an e-mail address in the To or CC list boxes, though, click on Address Book.

8 Once you've added entries to the Address Book, you can use those entries to address future e-mail messages. To do so, open the Compose Mail window as you normally would, click on Address Book, click on the listed names and the To and/or CC buttons as desired, and then click on OK.

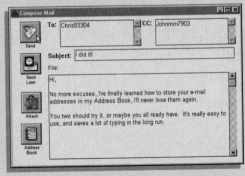

7 Click on OK to return to your now-addressed mail message. Complete and send the message as you normally would.

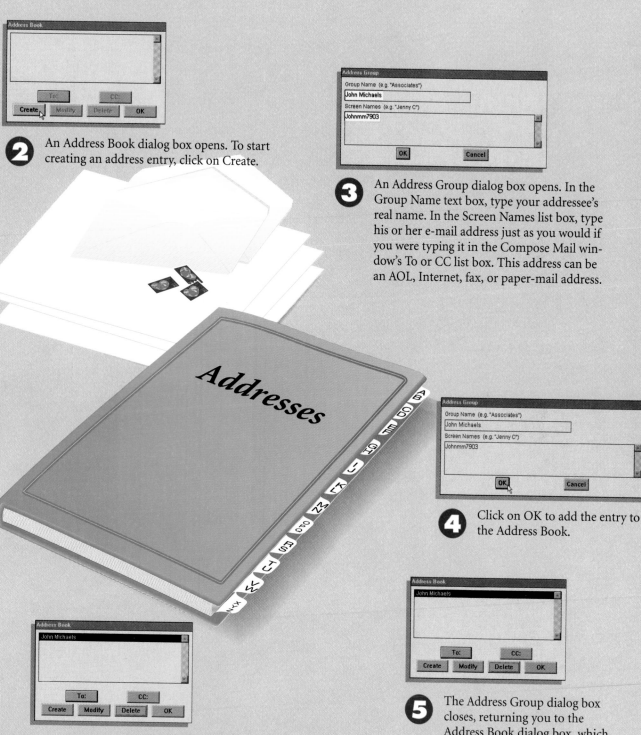

2 An Address Book dialog box opens. To start creating an address entry, click on Create.

3 An Address Group dialog box opens. In the Group Name text box, type your addressee's real name. In the Screen Names list box, type his or her e-mail address just as you would if you were typing it in the Compose Mail window's To or CC list box. This address can be an AOL, Internet, fax, or paper-mail address.

4 Click on OK to add the entry to the Address Book.

5 The Address Group dialog box closes, returning you to the Address Book dialog box, which now lists your acquaintance's real name as you typed it in the Group Name text box in step 3. To create additional addresses, repeat steps 2 through 4.

6 Now you can use the Address Book to address a mail message. Select the desired name, and then click on either To or CC. Clicking on To adds the corresponding e-mail address to the message's To list box; clicking on CC adds the address to the message's CC list box. To add multiple addresses to the message's To and/or CC list boxes, repeat this step as desired; the Address Book will automatically separate multiple addresses with the necessary commas.

TRY IT!

Here's a hands-on opportunity to practice some of the many techniques involved in sending and receiving mail messages on AOL. You'll use much of of what you've learned in the previous chapter, as well as some important techniques from earlier chapters. Chapter numbers are included in parentheses after each step to show you where we first introduced the technique required to perform that step. (**Note:** Before attempting this activity, be sure that you have installed AOL for Windows and set up your AOL online membership account. For details, see Chapter 3.)

If necessary, turn on your computer.

Start America Online for Windows. From your Windows Desktop click Start, point to Programs, then point to the America Online program group and click on the America Online item (Chapter 3).

Click on the
Flashbar's
Compose Mail icon to open the Compose
Mail window (Chapter 7).

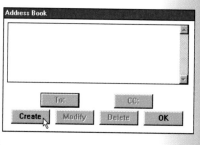

Click on
Address Book
to open the
Address Book
dialog box
(Chapter 7).

Click on
Create to
open the
Address
Group dialog
box (Chapter 7).

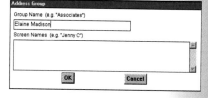

In the Group
Name text
box, type
your real
name (Chapter 7). Do not type the name
shown here.

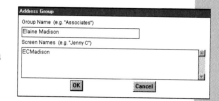

In the Screen
Names list
box, type
your screen
name (Chapter 7). Do not type the
screen name shown here.

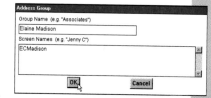

Click on OK
to close the
Address
Group dialog
box and return to the Address Book
dialog box (Chapter 7).

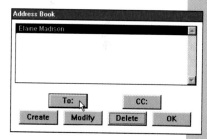

Click on your
name (if
necessary),
and then
click on To
(Chapter 7).

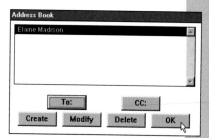

Click on OK
to close the
Address
Book dialog
box and re-
turn to the
Compose Mail window (Chapter 7).

Continue to next page ▶

TRY IT!

Continue below

11

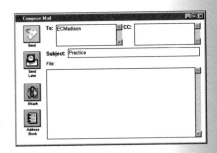

Verify that your screen name now appears in the Compose Mail window's To list box. Then, in the Subject text box, type **Practice** (Chapter 7).

12

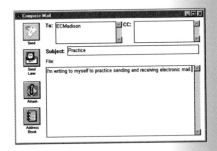

In the Compose Mail window's central list box, type **I'm writing to myself to practice sending and receiving electronic mail** (Chapter 7).

13

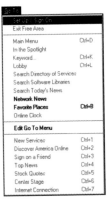

Choose Setup & Sign On from the Go To menu to move the Welcome window in front of the Compose Mail window (Chapter 7).

14

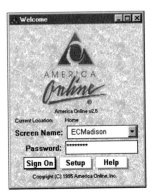

Verify that *your* screen name displays in the Screen Name drop-down list box. Then type your password in the Password text box (Chapter 3).

15

Click on Sign On (Chapter 3).

16

Wait a few moments as AOL for Windows dials your local access number, connects to AOL, checks your password, and then opens the online Welcome! window (Chapter 3).

17

Move the Compose Mail window in front of the Welcome! window (Chapter 7).

Click on
Send to send
your e-mail
message
(Chapter 7).

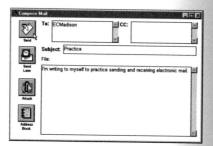

Click on OK
to close the
dialog box
that tells you your mail has been sent.
(Chapter 7)

When the red
flag on the
Flashbar's Read New Mail icon comes
up (which should be almost immediately), click on that icon to open the
New Mail window (Chapter 7).

Verify that
the message
you just sent
yourself is selected, and then click
on Read (Chapter 7).

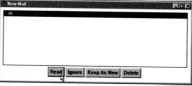

Examine the
message, and
then double-
click on the
message
window's
Control
Menu box to close the message window
(Chapter 2).

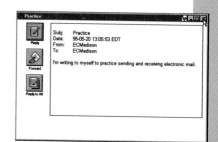

Choose Exit
from the File
menu
(Chapter 3).

Click on Exit
Application
to both sign
off from AOL and exit AOL for
Windows (Chapter 3).

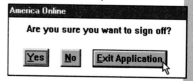

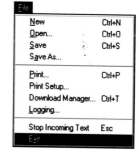

CHAPTER 8

Downloading Files

 In Chapter 7, you learned that you can download files that are attached to mail messages. But a bigger selection of files is also available to you online: AOL offers over 50,000 publicly available files—from games and graphics to diagnostic utilities and full-blown word processing programs. And except for your online charges, you can download any or all of these files for free!

You might question the legality of this. After all, it *is* illegal to upload or download copyrighted files without permission. Fortunately, both you and AOL already *have* this permission. Unlike the commercial software you might buy in a store, each of AOL's downloadable files are generally one of three special software types—freeware, shareware, or demoware—all of which can be uploaded, downloaded, or otherwise copied at will.

Freeware (also know as *public domain software*) is just what the name implies: software that's completely free. *Shareware* is software that you *try* for free, but for which you must pay a nominal fee (generally $2–$30) should you decide to use the software beyond the specified trial period. *Demoware* is generally a trimmed-down version of a larger commercial program, provided free as an enticement to buy the full-function version.

Regardless of price, much of this software is of surprisingly high quality that sometimes rivals or even surpasses its commercial counterparts. So take a chance, download a file or two, and see what no money can get you.

How to Search for and Download a File

A OL's downloadable files are organized into specialized file collections called *software libraries*. Software libraries can be found in every AOL department—usually indicated by buttons or list-box items that display a stack of floppy disks—and provide a good way to browse topic-specific files. These libraries are, however, by their very nature limited in scope and can sometimes be difficult to find. Rather than trying to work with these individual libraries, you can get central access to most downloadable files through *File Search*, AOL's searchable database of files. This page shows you how to search for files, and how to download a file once you've found it.

TIP SHEET

▶ Once you've downloaded a file, it's ready to use. If you're still relatively inexperienced with computers, ask a computer-savvy friend to show you how to locate and use this downloaded file. By default, the file will be found on your hard disk in the directory (a subsection of the disk) specified by the Download Manager window shown in step 5. This directory is usually c:\aol25\download.

▶ Don't be concerned if a file description indicates that you need an "UnZIPing" program. If the file ends with .ZIP or .ARC, AOL for Windows *is* your unZIPing program.

▶ If the file you're downloading contains a computer *image* (also known as a *picture* or *graphic*), step 6 may be slightly different. You might see an Image Transfer dialog box instead of the File Transfer dialog box, and you might see the image on screen as it downloads.

▶ Try using the keyword *software* to visit the Software Center, one of AOL's most popular file-library areas.

▶ **1** Make sure you're signed on to AOL, and then click on the Flashbar's File Search icon. (Or use the keyword **file search** or **quickfind**.) Be sure you are signed on using your own screen name. It's possible to sign onto AOL as a "Guest," but guests cannot download files.

8 When you're done using AOL, sign off without exiting AOL for Windows. (Choose Exit from the File menu, and then click on Yes.) If the file you downloaded ends with .ZIP or .ARC—indicating that the file is stored in a compressed format to save download time—this window will open to show what file or files ("members") have been extracted from the compressed file.

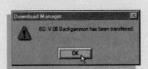

7 When the download is complete, a Download Manager dialog box opens to indicate this. Click on OK to close the dialog box.

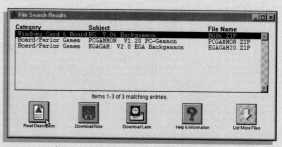

2 The File Search window opens. To get a list of the newest files, click on Past month or Past week at the top of the window; otherwise, leave All dates selected. To narrow the search, check one or more specific categories. To narrow the search even further, type a search criterion or criteria at the bottom of the window. (For more information on using search criteria, see Chapter 11.) When you're ready, click on List Matching Files.

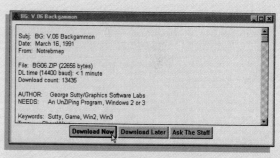

3 After a moment, a File Search Results window opens, listing the files that meet your search parameters. Scroll to find a file that interests you (using the List More Files button when it's available, to add files to the list). When you see one of interest, click on the file and then on Read Description. If you can't find a file that interests you, return to the File Search window and repeat step 2.

4 A detailed description of the selected file opens (you can maximize the description window, if desired). Read the description carefully. Pay close attention to the estimated time it will take to download the file, the computer equipment and/or software necessary to use the file, and the general description. If you want to download this file, click on Download Now. Otherwise, return to the File Search Results window and repeat step 3.

5 A Download Manager window opens, giving you the option to specify a different file name or disk location for the file. For now, just click on OK.

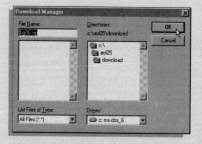

6 A File Transfer dialog box opens, displaying the progress of your file transfer (download).

How to Use the Download Manager

On the previous page, you learned how to download a single file. But what if you want to download more than one file at a time, or what if you don't want to start downloading files until after you've completed some other AOL exploration? In either case, you can call upon AOL's Download Manager to help. The Download Manager is essentially a to-do list, keeping track of every file you've decided to download. As you perform multiple file searches and/or explore multiple software libraries, you simply add files to the list. Then, when you're ready to download, you ask the Download Manager to download every selected file, all at once. This page shows you how.

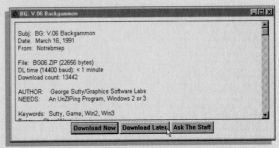

1 Once you've used File Search or a software library to locate and display the description of a file that you want to download, click on Download Later rather than on Download Now.

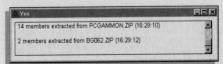

7 When you're done using AOL, sign off without exiting AOL for Windows. If any of the files you downloaded end with .ZIP or .ARC, the File Transfer Log window will show what file or files have been extracted from those compressed files. Your downloaded files are now ready to use.

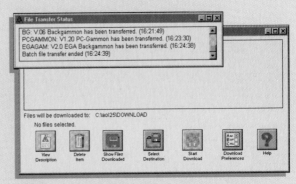

6 When the download is complete, the File Transfer dialog box closes automatically; the File Transfer Log and Download Manager windows remain open.

TIP SHEET

▶ **Once you've signed off from AOL, the Download Manager can still serve several purposes. Click on the Flashbar's Download Manager icon or choose Download Manager from the File menu to see a list of files that you've selected for downloading, but haven't yet downloaded. Click on Show Files Downloaded at this point, and you'll open a Files You've Downloaded list.**

▶ **If you accidentally sign off and exit AOL for Windows in one step after downloading a compressed file, AOL for Windows will *not* automatically decompress that file. To decompress this file manually, open the Files You've Downloaded list as described in the previous tip, click on the compressed file, and then click on Decompress.**

▶ **For lengthy downloads, check Sign Off After Transfer in step 5, and then turn your attention to other matters. AOL for Windows will then automatically download your files, sign off, and extract files as appropriate.**

The file has been added to your download list. To view your list or start the download, select 'Download Manager' below (or select from the File Menu or the Toolbar later).

OK   Download Manager

2 A dialog box informs you that the selected file has been added to your download list. Click on OK to close this dialog box.

3 Repeat steps 1 and 2 for each file that you want to download. Feel free to explore AOL between adding files to your download list. When you're finally ready to start the download, click on the Flashbar's Download Manager icon, or choose Download Manager from the File menu. (If you're ready to download immediately after adding the last file to your list, you can also click on Download Manager rather than on OK in step 2.)

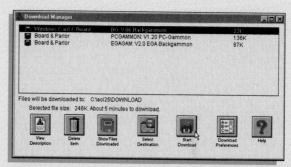

4 A Download Manager window opens, listing the files you've selected. Click on Start Download.

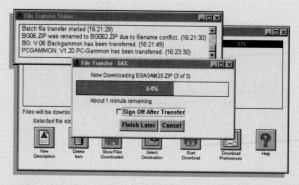

5 Next you'll see a File Transfer dialog box and a File Transfer Log window. The File Transfer dialog box displays the progress of your overall download, while the File Transfer Log window displays a download log. In the Download Manager window in the background, you may also be able to see the progress of each file as it's downloaded.

How to Upload a File

Got a great game? A really cool program? Why not share your favorite programs and graphics with other AOL members? Uploading is free and easy and it's one more way for you to contribute to the information on AOL. Just make sure the files you're uploading are Freeware or Shareware and send a complete set of files, including executables and any documentation, so the person who downloads it will find it as useful as you do.

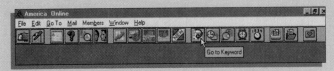

1 Make sure you're signed on to AOL, and then click on the Flashbar's Keyword icon. (Or choose Keyword from the Go To menu.)

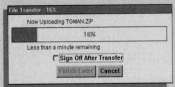

8 A File Transfer dialog box opens to display the progress of the file transfer from your computer to AOL. The length of this transfer will depend primarily on the file's size and your modem's baud rate. Once the file transfer is complete, another File Transfer dialog box will open to inform you of that fact. Click on the OK button to close this dialog box.

TIP SHEET

▸ **Compress all the files that go with a program into one compressed file; one file will take less time to upload and be easier for other users to download. If you need a compression program use the keyword SOFTWARE and check the "Helpful Utilities" library.**

▸ **Each file that is uploaded to AOL is checked by the forum librarians to ensure that it is not copyrighted, infected, or bug-ridden. Be patient, it may take a week or two for the library staff to let you know when the file is available to download.**

▸ **The time you spend uploading files is credited back to you so that upload time is actually free. The time you spend composing the file description is not free so you may want to write it on paper ahead of time to spend less time composing online.**

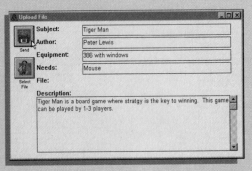

7 Click on send to begin the upload.

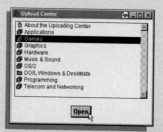

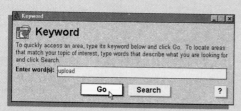

In the Keyword window type **upload** and click on Go.

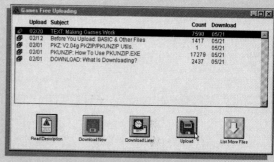

Choose the appropriate forum for your upload in the Upload Center list box and click on Open. (Or simply double-click on the forum.)

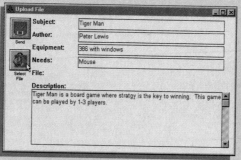

The forum's Free Uploading window will open. Click on upload.

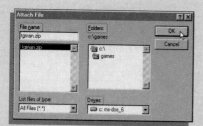

An Attach File dialog box opens. Use the Drives, Directories, and File name boxes as necessary to identify the file and indicate where is stored on your computer, then click on OK. (If you need help with drives and directories, consult your Windows documentation.)

Enter the information regarding your upload in the Upload File dialog box (do not enter the information listed here) and click on Select File.

CHAPTER 9

FlashSessions

 Ever wish you had more time? Tired of baby-sitting those file downloads and tying up your phone line? How about letting the computer do more work for you? In Chapter 7 you learned how to send and receive mail. In Chapter 8 we introduced you to file downloads. Now we'll show you how AOL and your computer can save you time and money by doing these and other tasks at night or while you're away from home, using *FlashSessions*.

This chapter will show you how to set up and schedule your own flashsessions.

Now when you have time to read your mail, it can be ready for you to review and respond to offline. AOL's working to make your busy schedule a little easier to manage.

How to Set Up a FlashSession

Setting up flashsessions is easy. AOL has designed the set-up screen with easy-to-use check boxes. All you need to do is determine how much of the mail, downloading, and news activities you want to use. Then turn them on or off with a click of your mouse. Everyone in your home can benefit from flashsessions.

▶ **1** Start AOL for Windows, but don't sign on to AOL. Choose FlashSessions from the Mail menu.

7 Your flashsession set up may be activated now or scheduled for a later time.

TIP SHEET

▶ **To send mail to AOL during a flashsession, use the Send Later button in the Compose Mail window. (See Chapter 7 for more information on composing mail.)**

▶ **Only Internet Newsgroup messages can be sent and retrieved during flashsessions. Use the Read Offline list to set up newsgroups for flashsessions. (Chapter 26 discusses Internet Newgroups.)**

6 Click OK to accept the screen names you have selected.

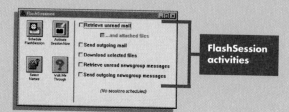

2 The FlashSessions window will open with scheduling icons and check boxes for flashsession activities.

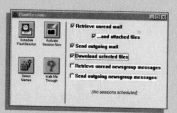

3 Determine which activities you want to occur during your flashsession and click on the check box next to each one. (Refer back to Chapter 2 for more information on using check boxes.) You may seen an "X" rather than a check mark in the box.

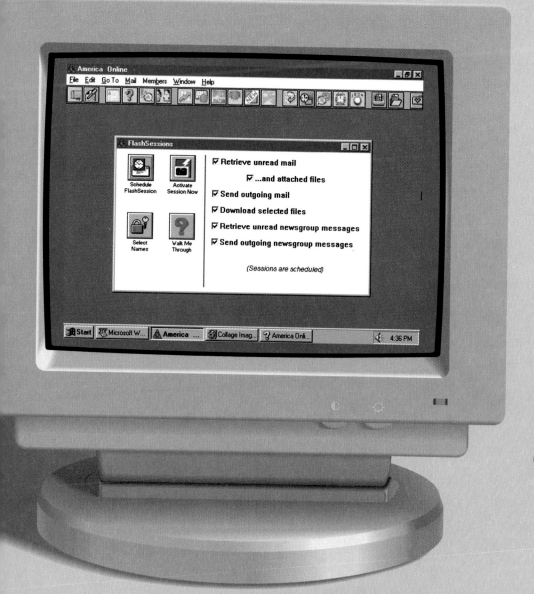

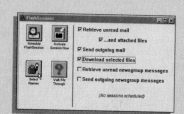

4 Click on the Select Names button.

5 Select the screen name(s) to be used during your flashsessions. Enter the appropriate password next to each screen name. (See Chapter 21 for more information on sharing your account with family members.)

How to Run a FlashSession Now

O nce you've set up your flashsession activities you can choose to run the flashsession at any time of the day, any day of the week. AOL gives you the option of scheduling your flash-sessions or running them immediately, even if you have a schedule set up. FlashSessions can always be run at your convenience!

▶ ❶ Choose Activate FlashSession Now from the Mail menu.

❼ When the flashsession is complete and you have been signed off AOL, the Goodbye! window will be displayed on your screen with the FlashSession Status window.

TIP SHEET

▶ **Each screen name has its own incoming mailbox, outgoing mail-box, and Download Manager.**

▶ **You can compose all your e-mail messages and Internet newsgroup messages offline, then activate a flashsession to sign on and send them.**

2 The Activate FlashSession Now window will open. If you need to check your flashsession settings, click on the Set Session button, otherwise skip to step 5.

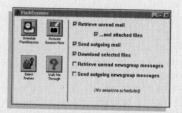

3 The FlashSessions window will open, and the activities that you have previously chosen will be marked in the check boxes. You may add or remove activities at this time by clicking on the check boxes. If you need to choose screen names, click on the Select Names icon. (See the previous pages for more information on the Select Names icon.)

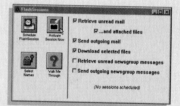

4 Once you have completed any necessary changes, click on the Activate Session Now box.

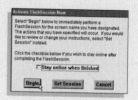

6 The Flashsession will sign you on to AOL, perform the designated activities, and sign off. A FlashSession status box will update as each activity is performed.

5 An Activate FlashSession Now window will open. Click on the Begin button to start your flashsession.

How to Run a FlashSession at a Scheduled Time

Now that you've set up your FlashSession activities, why not set the scheduler to run the flashsession at a time that is most convenient to you. Whether it is during the night while you're sleeping or during the day while you're at work, flashsessions will ensure that your mail and Internet newsgroups will be taken care of while you're busy with other matters. And you won't monopolize the phone line doing downloads when important calls may be coming in.

▶ **1** Choose FlashSessions from the Mail menu.

8 The FlashSessions window is now displayed. Note the window now reads "Sessions are scheduled." Make sure to leave your computer on with the AOL for windows software running so your flashsessions will take place as scheduled.

7 Click on the OK button when you are finished setting up your flashsession schedule.

2 If you have already designated your flashsession activities, click on the Schedule FlashSession icon. (If you have not chosen your flashsession activities, refer back in this chapter to How to Set Up a FlashSession.)

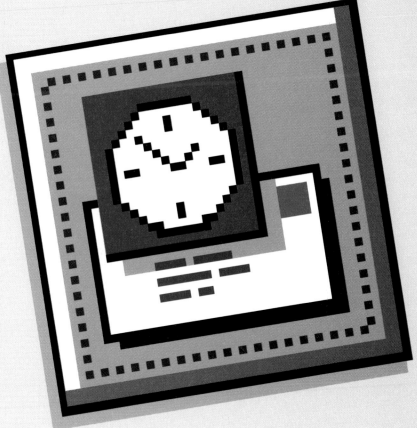

3 The Schedule FlashSessions window opens. Use the check boxes to select the day(s) on which you would like your flashsession(s) to occur.

4 In the Starting Time window set the time for your first flashsession to occur. Use the up and down arrows to set the time in hours, then click on the drop-down list to set minutes. (Time is set based on the 24-hour clock.)

6 Click on the Enable Scheduler box to activate your selections.

5 Click on the drop-down list in the How Often window to set the frequency for your flashsessions.

How to Read Mail and Downloaded Files from FlashSessions

All screen names listed under your account have their own Personal Filing Cabinet to help keep track of FlashSession downloads, incoming and outgoing mail, and incoming and outgoing Internet newsgroup messages. The Personal Filing Cabinet can be customized for each individual screen name by using the mouse to Drag and Drop the files and folders in their own area.

▶ **1** Choose Personal Filing Cabinet from the Mail menu.

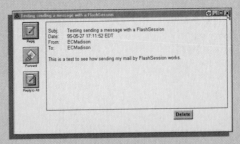

6 To close the mail message window, click on the windows close button (refer to Chapter 2).

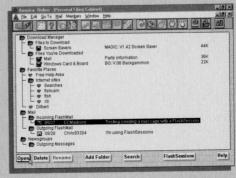

5 To read your mail, select the mail message (from either the Incoming or Outgoing FlashMail folders) and click on Open, or double-click on the message.

TIP SHEET

▶ **Use the Add Folder button to create new folders in your Incoming Flashmail folder to sort your mail messages by subject.**

▶ **Incoming Flashmail may also be read by choosing Read Incoming Mail from the Mail menu.**

▶ **Outgoing Flashmail may also be read by choosing Read Outgoing Mail from the Mail menu.**

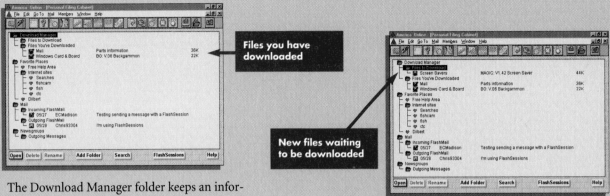

Files you have downloaded

New files waiting to be downloaded

2 The Download Manager folder keeps an information list of the files that you have downloaded or have selected to download. Downloaded files must be opened from the directory to which you downloaded them, usually C:\Aol25\download.

3 As you select files to download, the file information is added to the Files to Download folder under Download Manager.

4 The Mail folder holds all of your Incoming and Outgoing *Flashmail* (mail sent and received during FlashSessions).

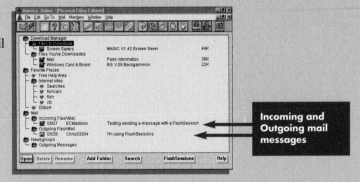

Incoming and Outgoing mail messages

CHAPTER 10

Chatting

 As we mentioned at the beginning of Chapter 6, AOL is an electronic community comprising AOL's many members. You've already seen two of the three primary ways to communicate with fellow members of this community: message boards and mail.

In this chapter, we'll show you a third way to communicate: *chatting*. Unlike message boards and mail, chatting is immediate, or *real-time*. Chatting is the electronic equivalent of a face-to-face or telephone conversation; there's virtually no lag time between sending a message and receiving a response.

So how does this chatting thing work? Well, anytime you're online—even if it's in the middle of the night—you can be sure that there are other AOL members online at the same time. To start chatting, you first enter one of AOL's many *chat rooms*. Once you're in a chat room, you type and send a message, and everyone in that room immediately sees that message. Because there can be up to 23 members in any one chat room, it's only a matter of seconds before you find yourself involved in a real-time conversation.

If you've never chatted online before, it may seem somewhat strange at first, but do give it a try. Chatting is one of the best ways to meet new people, expose yourself to new ideas, and generally become more involved with your electronic community.

How to Chat

AOL has dozens of different chat rooms. Most of them focus on a specific subject, but no matter what chat room you visit, the *techniques* for chatting are pretty much the same. If you're new to chatting, one of the best chat rooms to visit first is the Lobby, a chat room without any specific focus. Like a hotel lobby, AOL's Lobby is usually full of people going from one place to another, and a few are usually willing to linger a while and have a conversation. This page will show you how to visit the Lobby and how to chat.

1 Make sure you're signed on to AOL, and then click on the Flashbar's People Connection icon. (Or choose Lobby from the Go To menu.)

▶ **In a roomful of people, it's easy to get lost in a sea of multiple conversations. Until you get used to chatting, be patient and try to stick to a single conversation.**

▶ **When you enter a chat room, you may be greeted by a person whose screen name starts with "Guide." This person is an *online guide*—a fellow member who volunteers to stay in a particular room, greet new entrants, and provide help as necessary. If you have any questions about chatting, ask your online guide.**

▶ **You may find that some chat messages include *online shorthands* such as ":)" and "LOL." (Online shorthands are also commonly used on message boards and in e-mail.) To learn more about online shorthands, click on PC Studio, double-click on What's Happening This Week, and then double-click on Online Shorthands.**

▶ **The Lobby is only one of AOL's many chat rooms. Visiting other chat rooms is covered later in this chapter.**

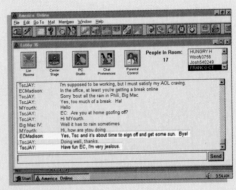

8 When you're done chatting, be polite by sending out a good-bye message. Wait a few moments for other members' good-bye responses, and then close the Lobby window.

7 Continue to receive and send messages as desired. Remember to be polite; a lot of people will see what you write.

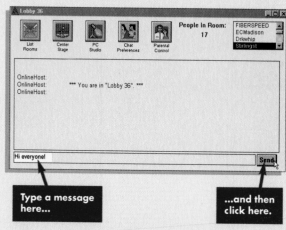

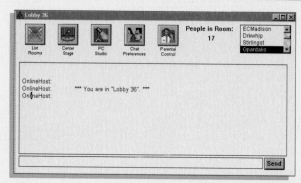

2 A Lobby window opens, and the automated OnlineHost greets you by telling you what Lobby you are in. If the original Lobby is full (23 members) you may find yourself in an alternate Lobby, such as Lobby 1, Lobby 2, and so on. No matter—every Lobby works the same.

3 In the long text box at the bottom of the Lobby window, type a greeting message. Then click on Send. (As with messages on message boards and e-mail, avoid using uppercase—it's like shouting.)

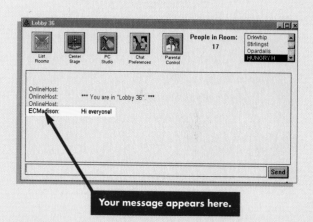

4 Your screen name appears in the window's central list box, followed by your message.

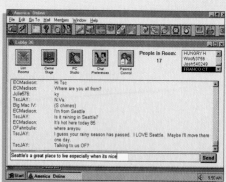

6 When someone responds to you, respond in turn by typing a message in that long text box, and then clicking on Send again. To indicate whom you're responding to (out of the possible 23 room occupants), be sure to include that member's screen name—or some abbreviation thereof—in your response. (Uppercase *is* acceptable when it's part of someone's screen name.)

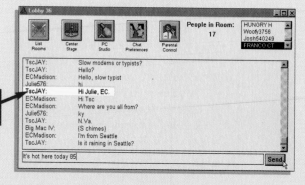

5 Within seconds, you'll see someone else's message appear in the list box. They may be responding to you, sending out a general greeting, or talking to someone else. Keep in mind that you've just entered a roomful of people who may be already involved in a conversation.

How to Share Personal Information with a Chat Partner

If you're like many people, you prefer to learn a little bit about another person before diving too deeply into a face-to-face *or* electronic conversation. But if you're starting an online conversation, it can take a lot of time to ask a person about his or her real name, hobbies, occupation, and so on. Enter the *member profile*. A member profile is an online personal-information form that many members fill out for use by other members. If your online chat partner has filled out a member profile, you can look at that profile to gain some insight into your partner. Ideally, you'll find some things you have in common; after all, isn't that how most friendships start?

TIP SHEET

▶ **You can share profiles in any chat room, not just the Lobby. You'll learn more about other chat rooms later in this chapter.**

▶ **You can also look up a member's profile by choosing Get a Member's Profile from the Members menu.**

▶ **Notice that the window shown in step 6 also provides a Message button. This button enables you to send an *Instant Message*—a chat message that only your recipient can see—to anyone in your current chat room. You can also send an Instant Message to almost anyone else who's currently online, by choosing Send an Instant Message from the Members menu.**

▶ **If someone sends you an Instant Message, an Instant Message window will open automatically, showing you both the message and the sender's screen name. From this window, you can easily respond with an Instant Message of your own, by clicking on Respond in the Instant Message window.**

▶ **1** Before you start looking at other people's member profiles, it's polite first to complete one yourself. To fill out your own profile, make sure you're signed on to AOL, and then choose Edit Your Online Profile from the Members menu.

8 Now you can talk about some of the things you have in common. It's a great way to start cementing your new friendship!

7 If the person has filled out a member profile, that profile will display in a Member Profile window. (If he or she hasn't filled out a member profile, a dialog box informs you that no profile is available.) Read the profile, and then return to the Lobby; your chat partner should arrive back at about the same time.

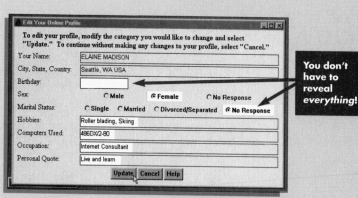

You don't have to reveal *everything*!

2 The Edit Your Online Profile window opens, offering several text boxes and radio buttons that you can use to describe yourself. The Your Name and City, State, Country boxes are filled in for you already.

3 You're not *required* to share personal information that you'd rather not reveal, so complete only those parts of your profile that you care to, and then click on Update.

4 A dialog box informs you that your profile has been created. Click on OK to close this dialog box.

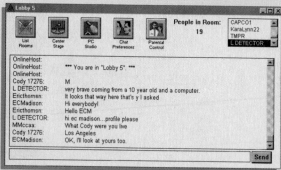

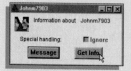

6 A window bearing that person's screen name opens. Click on Get Info.

5 Now that you've filled out your own profile, you can start looking at another person's profile with a clear conscience. To do so, move to the Lobby and start a conversation with someone. If you decide you'd like to learn more about your chat partner, invite your partner to take a moment to "share profiles." (You *can* peek at someone's profile secretly, but it's much more fun to *share* profiles.) To see a profile, find and double-click on the person's screen name in the list box in the Lobby window's upper-right corner.

How to Customize Your Chat Sessions

Once you've become accustomed to chatting you may find the need to customize your Chat sessions. AOL has created Chat Preferences for just this purpose. Now when you find that you'd like to know who's coming and going from your Chat Room or you'd like to have the messages double-spaced, just set your chat preferences. You can even alphabetize the member list, and if you find someone's messages annoying or obnoxious, AOL has a solution for that too!

1 Make sure you're signed on to AOL, and then click on the Flashbar's People Connection icon. (Or choose Lobby from the Go To menu.)

6 Once you have marked the Ignore box on the person's screen name, you will no longer see the messages sent by that person during your chat session.

TIP SHEET

▸ **You may change your personal Chat Preferences from any Chat Room at anytime.**

▸ **The default settings of the *Notify Me When Members Arrive/Leave*, *Double-Space Incoming Messages*, and *Alphabetize The Member List* preferences are in the off position.**

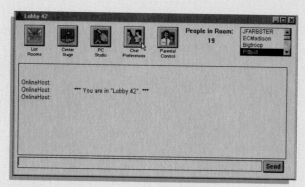

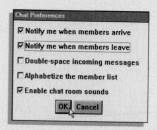

2 A Lobby window opens. Click on the Chat Preferences icon. (Skip to step 5 to use the Ignore feature.)

3 A Chat Preferences window opens. Select your preferences by clicking on the check box next to the item.

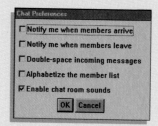

4 When you have completed selecting your preferences, click on OK to close the window. Your chat preferences are now set. Continue on to step 5 to learn how to use the Ignore feature.

5 If you are in a room where you find a member's comments uncomfortable, find and double-click on the person's screen name in the list box in the window's upper-right corner. A window bearing that person's screen name opens; click on the Ignore check box. To close the window use the window's close button (refer to Chapter 2).

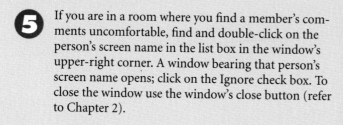

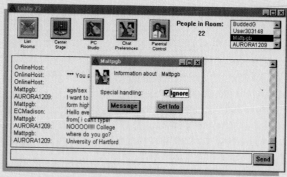

How to Visit Other Chat Rooms

When you visit the Lobby, you've actually stepped into the entranceway of AOL's People Connection department, which is entirely dedicated to chatting. From within the Lobby, you can visit just about any other chat room. AOL's chat rooms fall into three categories: *public rooms*, which are permanent rooms that AOL has set up to address a variety of member interests; *member rooms*, which are temporary public rooms that members create to discuss a topic not addressed by an existing public room; and *private rooms*, which are temporary rooms that members create to discuss topics privately.

TIP SHEET

▶ You can't visit a room that's already filled to its 23-member capacity—at least, not until someone leaves.

▶ If you still can't find a room to suit you, try creating your *own* room. To do so, click on Create Room or Private Room (where available), provide a name for your room, and then click on Create or Go. Rooms you create through the Create Room button will automatically appear in the Member Rooms window, and anyone can visit. Rooms created through the Private Room button, however, are more restricted; only those members who know when and under what name your private room exists can join you there.

▶ If you're a parent who wants to let one of your children share your AOL account, you may be concerned about the focus of certain chat rooms, especially those created by other members. Fortunately, you can prevent your children from visiting certain rooms. See Chapter 21 to learn how.

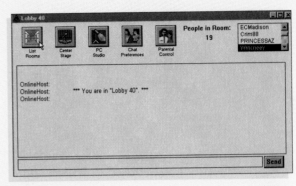

1 Go to the Lobby (see "How to Chat" earlier in this chapter), and then click on List Rooms.

8 When you want to move from your new room to another room, click once again on the List Rooms button.

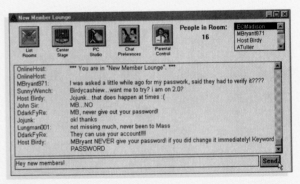

7 Regardless of what type of room you enter, the automated OnlineHost greets you by telling you what room you are in. Your new room window probably looks and works exactly as it did in the Lobby; you may even see some leftover Lobby conversation. Once you've arrived in a room, introduce yourself and start chatting, just as you would if you were in the Lobby. Remember, though, that if your new room has a specific focus, you should try to stick to the topic at hand.

2 An Active Public Rooms window opens, listing every *active* public room—that is, every public room that currently contains members. To visit an active public room, scroll through the list box until you find a room that interests you, click on that room, click on Go, and then skip to step 7. (If the More button is active, you can use this button to add more active public rooms to the list.) To check out other room options instead, continue on to step 3.

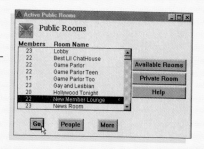

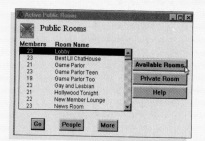

3 Click on Available Rooms.

4 The Available Rooms window opens, listing every available public room— that is, every public room that's currently empty. To visit an empty public room (thus making it an *active* public room), scroll through the list box until you find a room that interests you, click on that room, click on Open, and then skip to step 7. (If the More button is active, you can use this button to add more available public rooms to the list.) To check out other room options instead, continue on to step 5.

5 Click on Member Rooms.

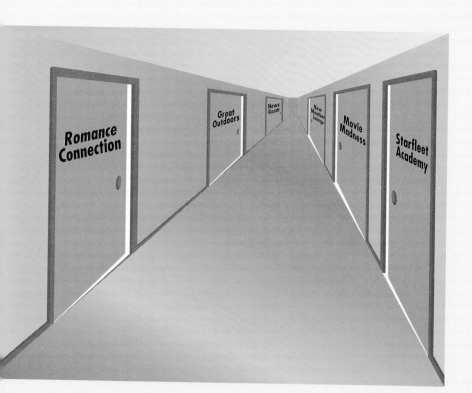

6 The Member Rooms window opens, listing every available member room. To visit a member room, scroll through the list box until you find a room that interests you, click on that room, click on Open, and then continue on to step 7. (If the More button is active, you can use this button to add more available public rooms to the list.)

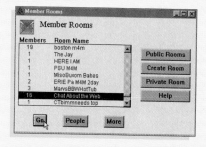

CHAPTER 11

Searchable Databases

We've already mentioned searchable databases several times throughout this book. In Chapter 4, we introduced you to the very basics of working with a searchable database called the Directory of Services. In Chapter 7, we told you that you can find another member's screen name by using a searchable database, the Member Directory. In Chapter 8, you learned how to access downloadable files through another searchable database, File Search.

Clearly, the searchable database is a pretty common AOL feature. But what *is* a searchable database, and how do you search one?

A *database* is simply a collection of related information, and electronic databases are quite common in the computer world. How you search a searchable database depends both on the database and on the information you're trying to find. The basic search techniques, however, are common among all AOL searchable databases and among all searches. This chapter will show you those techniques.

How to Search a Searchable Database

In Chapter 4, you learned the fundamentals of searching a searchable database: You type a search criterion, and then click on List Articles for a list of articles that meet your criterion. This type of basic search works well in some circumstances, but isn't very efficient in others. For example, if you search AOL's News Search database using the criterion "politics," AOL might list hundreds of articles. In cases like this, you'll want to narrow your search and get a much shorter, more precise list—by using a more specific criterion and/or by specifying multiple criteria. This page shows you how.

▶ **①** Searchable databases are available all over AOL. For central access to these databases, however, proceed directly to AOL's Reference Desk. To move to the Reference Desk, click on the Main menu from the Welcome! window and then click on Reference. (Or click on the Flashbar's Keyword icon, and use the Keyword **reference**.)

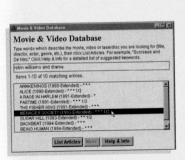

⑧ Once the list is down to a manageable size, double-click on any article that interests you.

⑦ If your multiple criteria produces the short list you need, skip to step 8. If your list is still too long, repeat steps 5 and/or 6, using additional or more specific criteria. If your criteria has narrowed your search *too* much, however, a dialog box like this one will tell you that no matches have been found. Click on OK to close the dialog box, and then repeat steps 5 and/or 6 using *less* specific criteria and *fewer* total criteria.

TIP SHEET

▸ If no List Articles button is available, click on whatever appropriately named button *is* available.

▸ The word *"and"* is only one of three available multiple search tools; the other two are *"or"* and *"not"*. Use *or* to broaden your search to items that match *any* criteria; use *"not"* to reverse your search to articles that *don't* match a criterion. For example, *"dogs or cats"* would find articles about dogs, about cats, or about both; *"dogs not cats"* would find articles about dogs, unless the articles were also about cats.

▸ You can mix and match search tools freely, but your total search phrase cannot exceed 45 characters, including spaces.

▸ Before searching a database, consider clicking on the search window's Help & Info button to get information specific to that database. For example, by clicking on the Movie & Video Database window's Help & Info button, you will see that you can search for G-rated movies by using the criterion *MPAAG*.

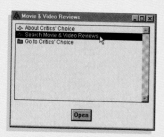

2 The Reference Desk window opens, providing a lengthy list of searchable databases. Scroll through the list until you find a database that interests you, and then double-click on that database.

3 If the next window that opens looks similar to the search window pictured in step 4, then skip to step 4. Otherwise, you may get a window or a series of windows like this one, which gives you some more choices along the way. Double-click on the likeliest choice in each window (usually any choice that includes the word *search*) until a search window opens (see the one pictured in step 4).

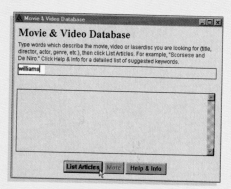

4 It's usually best to start out with a fairly general criterion first, just to see how many items are available within that general area. Type that criterion in the text box at the top of the search window, and then click on List Articles.

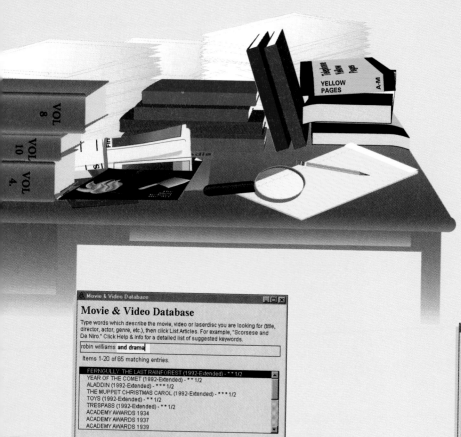

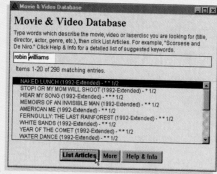

6 If your more specific criterion produces a list that is short enough for you, skip to step 8. Otherwise, repeat step 5 using an even more specific criterion—or consider using multiple criteria. To use multiple criteria, type in two or more individual criterion separated by the word *and*. Then, click again on List Articles.

5 If your general criterion produces a short list, then skip to step 8. Otherwise, narrow your search. Type a more specific criterion, and then click again on List Articles.

TRY IT!

Here's a hands-on opportunity to practice some of the many techniques involved in searching for and downloading files and using flash-sessions. In this exercise, you'll use many of the techniques you've read about in Chapters 8, 9 and 11, as well as some important techniques from earlier chapters. Chapter numbers are included in parentheses at the end of each step to show you where we first introduced the technique required to perform that step. (Note: Before attempting this activity, be sure that you have installed AOL for Windows and have set up your AOL membership account. For details, see Chapter 3.)

1

If necessary, switch on your computer.

2

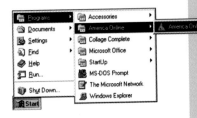

Start America Online for Windows. From your Windows Desktop click Start, point to Programs, then point to the America Online program group and click on the America Online item (*Chapter 3*).

3

Verify that your screen name (not the one shown here) is displayed in the Screen Name drop-down list box, and then type your password in the Password text box (*Chapter 3*).

4

Click on Sign On (*Chapter 3*).

5

Wait a few moments as AOL for Windows dials your local access number, connects to AOL, checks your password, and then opens the online Welcome! window (*Chapter 3*).

6

Click on the Flashbar's File Search icon, or use the keyword **file search** (*Chapter 8*).

7

In the File Search window, type **screen savers and magic**, and then click on List Matching Files (*Chapter 8*).

8

In the File Search Results window, click on the file item that ends with MAGIC142.ZIP, if necessary, and then click on Read Description (*Chapter 8*).

9

Maximize the description window, read the file description, and then click on Download Later (*Chapters 2 and 8*).

Continue to next page ▶

TRY IT!

Continue
below

13

Click on No
to close this
dialog box (*Chapter 8*).

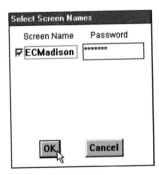

10

Click on OK
to close this dialog box (*Chapter 8*).

The file has been added to your download list. To view your list or start the download, select 'Download Manager' below (or select from the File Menu or the Toolbar later).

OK   Download Manager

14

Choose
FlashSessions
from the Mail
menu
(*Chapter 9*).

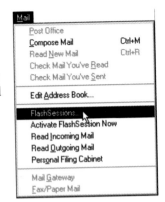

Mail
Post Office
Compose Mail   Ctrl+M
Read New Mail   Ctrl+R
Check Mail You've Read
Check Mail You've Sent

Edit Address Book...

FlashSessions...
Activate FlashSession Now
Read Incoming Mail
Read Outgoing Mail
Personal Filing Cabinet

Mail Gateway
Fax/Paper Mail

11

Choose Exit
from the File
menu
(*Chapter 3*).

File
New   Ctrl+N
Open...   Ctrl+O
Save   Ctrl+S
Save As...

Print...   Ctrl+P
Print Setup...
Download Manager... Ctrl+T
Logging...

Stop Incoming Text Esc
Exit

15

Click on the
Download
selected files
check box,
then click on
the Select
Names icon (*Chapter 9*).

FlashSessions
Schedule FlashSession
Activate Session Now
Select Names
Walk Me Through

☐ Retrieve unread mail
☐ ...and attached files
☐ Send outgoing mail
☑ Download selected files
☐ Retrieve unread newsgroup messages
☐ Send outgoing newsgroup messages

(No sessions scheduled)

12

Click on Yes
to sign off
from AOL
without exiting AOL for Windows
(*Chapter 3*).

America Online

Are you sure you want to sign off?

Yes   No   Exit Application

16

Click on the
check box
next to your
screen name
and type
your pass-
word in the
password
window. Click OK to close the Select
Screen Names window (*Chapter 9*).

Select Screen Names

Screen Name   Password
☑ ECMadison   *******

OK   Cancel

Click on
the Activate
Session Now
icon
(*Chapter 9*).

Click on the
Begin button
(*Chapter 9*).

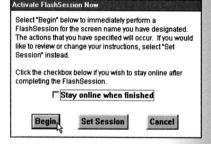

Wait a few moments while the
FlashSession signs you on to AOL and
begins your file transfer (*Chapter 9*).

The File
Transfer win-
dow displays
the progress
of your download (*Chapter 8*).

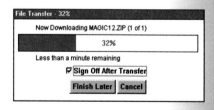

The
FlashSession
Status win-
dow will be displayed on your screen
describing your flashsession. Use the
windows Close button to close this
dialog box (*Chapters 2 and 9*).

22

The file you just downloaded,
MAGIC142.ZIP is a customizable
screensaver for Windows that draws
colorful patterns on your computer
monitor.

CHAPTER 12

Keeping Up with the News

You're probably used to getting most of your news from newspapers, magazines, television, and radio. These are all good news sources, but each has its drawbacks. Newspapers and magazines generally provide good, in-depth news coverage, but by their very nature they contain news that may be anywhere from many hours to many months old. Both television and radio can provide up-to-the-minute news, but these stories tend to be short because of limited air time.

Also, the amount of advertising carried by most newspapers, magazines, and television and radio stations can be overwhelming. In fact, sometimes there are more ads than news.

Enter AOL. Its news is substantial and up-to-date, available 24 hours a day, and ad-free. Plus, it's easy and fun to use. This chapter covers two of AOL's many news offerings, Today's News and Weather Forecasts.

So the next time you want to catch up on the news, leave that newspaper on the porch, put down the remote control, and reach instead for your keyboard and mouse. Your newest (and perhaps soon-to-be favorite) news source is only a few keystrokes and mouse clicks away.

How to Read Today's News

So you're interested in reading today's news articles. Are you interested in general news, or perhaps something more specific, such as business, sports, or entertainment news? Or maybe national or world news is more to your liking. No problem; AOL is ready for you on all counts. Whenever you're online, the top news is only a click away.

1 Make sure you're signed on to AOL, and then click on the Flashbar's Today's News icon. (Or choose Today's News from the Go To menu.)

6 To read another article, close the current article window, and repeat steps 3 through 5.

TIP SHEET

▶ **The Welcome! window that opens when you first sign on to AOL may contain a button for accessing today's news stories. If you prefer, you probably can use this button instead of doing step 1. Today's News is also on the Main menu.**

▶ **To print or save a news article for offline use, open the article's window, and then click on the Flashbar's Print or Save icon. These two icons work not only for saving and printing news articles, but for just about any AOL window that contains text.**

▶ **To see a listing of highlighted areas and features for the US & World, Business, Entertainment, Sports, and Weather icons, click on the Index button.**

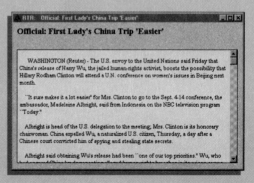

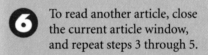

5 The selected article displays in its own window. Scroll as necessary to read it.

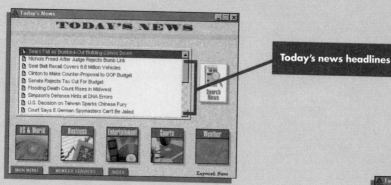

Today's news headlines

2 The Today's News window opens with a list box containing headlines of today's news articles and several news icons. To read an article in the list box, skip to step 4.

Click on any of these buttons...

...to change this list of headlines.

3 If you're looking for news on a specific topic click the icon for US & World, Business, Entertainment, Sports, or Weather. This will change the list of headlines accordingly. Or click on the Search News icon to access a searchable database of news articles. (Searchable databases are discussed in Chapter 11.)

4 Whether you're looking at the Today's News listing of headlines or a more specific listing, scroll through the list box as necessary to find an article that interests you. Once you do, double-click on that article's headline.

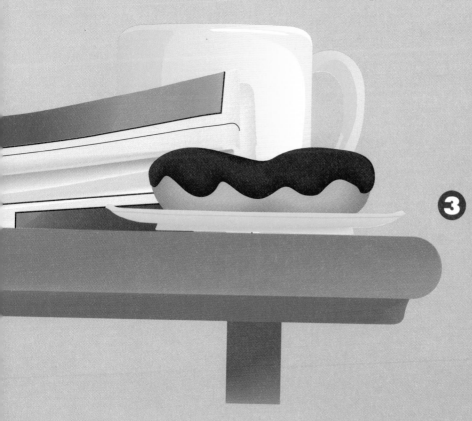

How to Check a Weather Forecast

Is it going to rain tomorrow? What kind of weather can you expect on your upcoming weekend trip? Weather information can be very critical to you at times. To see general weather forecasts for your area or vacation destination, you will want to frequent AOL's Weather area. There you'll find five-day weather forecasts for just about every major city in the world, and these forecasts are available 24 hours a day. So the next time you're wondering whether you should walk out of the house in a slicker or a swimsuit, ask AOL.

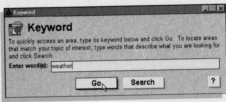

▶ **1** Make sure you're signed on to AOL, and then use the keyword **weather**. (Or click on the Flashbar's Today's News icon, and then double-click on Weather.)

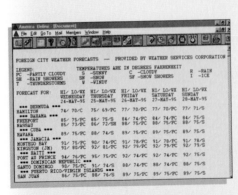

8 A weather forecast window opens, listing five-day forecasts for your selected area's major cities. Scroll as necessary to see the desired forecast.

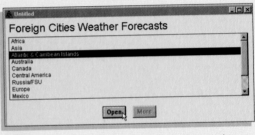

7 Another window opens, listing various countries, continents, and regions around the world. Scroll as necessary, click on the desired country, continent, or region, and then click on Open. (Or double-click on the desired country, continent, or region.)

TIP SHEET

▶ **To make weather forecasts easier to read, try maximizing the forecast window as we have done in steps 5 and 8. (Chapter 2 shows you how to maximize windows.)**

▶ **As you can see in step 2, AOL's weather area offers more than just general weather forecasts. You can also check ski reports, weather-related news, and many different types of weather maps. You can even discuss the weather with other AOL members. This is typical of AOL: a little something for everyone.**

2 The Weather window opens with several icons and a list box of various options for retrieving weather information. To check a weather forecast for a U.S. city, click on the U.S. Cities Forecast button. To check a forecast for a foreign city, skip to step 6.

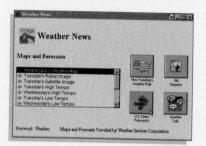

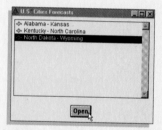

3 The U.S. Cities Forecasts window opens. Instead of making you scroll through a list of 50 states, the list box contains just a few alphabetized state groups. Click on the group that contains the desired state, and then click on Open. (Or double-click on the state group.)

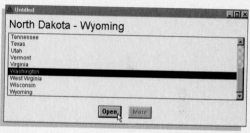

4 Another window opens, listing just those states contained in the group you chose in step 3. Scroll as necessary, click on the desired state, and then click on Open. (Or double-click on the state.)

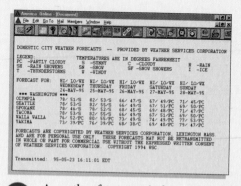

6 To check a weather forecast for a foreign city, scroll through the list box to find the Foreign Cities Forecast item and then double-click.

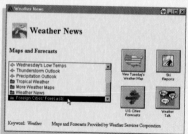

5 A weather forecast window opens, listing five-day forecasts for your selected state's major cities. Scroll as necessary to see the desired forecast. To also see a weather forecast for a foreign city, return to the Weather window shown in step 2 (close windows as necessary, or choose Weather from the Window menu), and then continue on to step 6. Otherwise, you can skip the rest of this activity.

CHAPTER 13

Newsstand

We've already discussed how to get today's news and search through the collections of electronic information that AOL has online. In this chapter we're going to introduce you to another collection of information, AOL's Newsstand. The Newsstand department gives you access to information on topics in a form you're already familiar with: your favorite magazines. From world news to sports to hobbies and education, AOL has magazines for every member of your family.

Just like the magazines at your local newsstand, each publication has its own special features and highlights. In addition, many magazines add extra features to their newsstand areas. Imagine discussing issues with their editors and writers, or searching through a magazine's searchable database for an interesting article you may have missed. There are also message boards, special activities, promotions, and even shopping!

So the next time you're going out to pick up your favorite magazine, go to your computer instead and read it online.

How to Read an Online Magazine

One reason magazines are such popular information sources is that they are so specialized. Thousands of different magazines are published each month, on subjects ranging from airplanes to zymurgy. You might read only one or two articles in your daily newspaper, but your monthly juggling journal is probably ragged because you read *every* article. On AOL you can read dozens of the most popular magazines—on line. And if you don't see your favorite magazine there yet, just wait. Online magazines offer many of the same advantages as other online news sources: 24-hour availability, up-to-date information, and so on. Who knows? Maybe you'll never have to pay for a magazine subscription again!

TIP SHEET

▶ **Many magazines have a Favorite Places icon to help you return to a special area. Just drag the magazine's Favorite Places icon to the Flashbar's Favorite Places icon. The next time you want to read the magazine, just click on the Flashbar's Favorite Places icon and then click on the magazine.**

▶ **Because of their varying specialties, you can also find magazines located in various AOL departments and areas that cover particular subjects. The Newsstand area simply makes many magazines easier to find.**

▶ **Some magazines offer their own message boards and searchable databases. To learn more about using message boards, see Chapter 6. To learn more about using searchable databases, see Chapter 11.**

▶ **1** Make sure you're signed on to AOL, and then click on Newsstand in the Main menu. (Or click on the Flashbar's Keyword icon and use the Keyword **newsstand**.)

8 To read another magazine article, return to the starting magazine window, and then repeat steps 5 through 7. To switch to another magazine, return to The Newsstand window (shown in steps 2 and 3), and repeat steps 3 through 7.

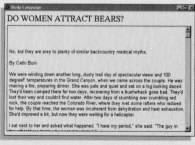

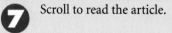

7 Scroll to read the article.

2 The Newsstand window opens, listing many of AOL's magazines and newspapers. For easier access, some of the most popular or newly available magazines and newspapers may also appear on their own buttons.

3 Scroll as necessary, and then double-click on the desired magazine. Or, click on the magazine's button if one is available.

4 Just as every printed magazine is different, so is every online magazine window. Typical online magazine windows, however, include a list box that serves as an electronic table of contents. Most windows also display buttons that enable you to do anything from learning more about the magazine to sending an electronic letter to the editor.

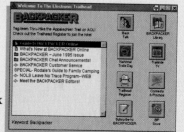

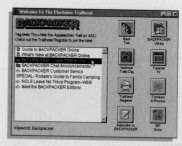

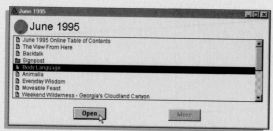

5 To read a magazine article, your best bet is to scroll through the list box to find something that interests you, and then double-click on that item. (If you prefer to be a bit more daring, go ahead and click on one of the buttons; there's no telling where one might take you.)

6 Another window opens, displaying either a magazine article or another list box. If the window displays an article, you can proceed to step 7. If the window displays a list box, scroll as necessary to find an item that interests you, select that item, and then click on Open. (If an Open button isn't available, then double-click on the list item instead.) Repeat this step as necessary until an article window opens.

How to Read *TIME* Online

TIME Magazine offers its online readers many special features, including their current U.S. and International editions, and *TIME* Daily, which provides *TIME's* view of today's late news. If you miss an issue, just use their searchable database to pick up the information you need.

TIME also offers several message boards organized by subject where you can meet with *TIME* writers and editors to discuss current events. You can even attend real-time online interviews with newsmakers, authors, and *TIME* staffers in *TIME's* Press Conference area.

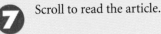 Scroll through the Newsstand list box as necessary and double-click on *TIME* Magazine. (Or click on the *TIME* icon if available.)

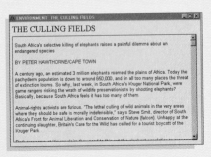

7 Scroll to read the article.

TIP SHEET

▶ *TIME* can also be accessed using the keyword TIME.

▶ To search past issues, click on the Service Center & Archives icon then double-click on Search Past Issues. Use keywords to search this searchable database (refer to Chapter 11).

▶ Click on the What's Hot icon to find *TIME* Daily and information on Press Conferences.

2 The *TIME* Magazine window opens. The list box is an electronic table of contents for the articles in this week's issue. The buttons around the list box enable you to use *TIME's* special features.

Special features

Double-click on an article here.

3 To read an article from this week's U.S. issue of *TIME* scroll through the list box as necessary to find one that interests you and then double-click on that item. Skip to step 7.

4 To read an article from the international issue of *TIME* click on the Time International icon.

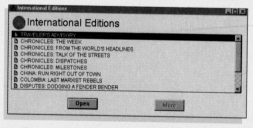

5 An International Editions window opens with a list box displaying magazine articles.

6 Scroll as necessary to select an article which interests you and double-click on the item.

How to Read *Consumer Reports* Online

Consumer Reports on AOL provides product and services reviews, ratings and advice—just like the printed edition. *Consumer Reports* on AOL offers collections of reports on autos, food and health, products and services for your home, electronics, and advice on personal-finance issues.

So next time youíre ready to buy something or need information on a product, there's no need to run to the corner for a magazine—read Consumer Reports on AOL.

▶ **1** Scroll through the Newsstand list box as necessary and double-click on Consumer Reports. (Or click on the Flashbar's Keyword icon and use the keyword **Consumer Reports**.)

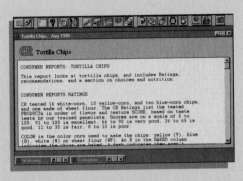

6 Scroll to read the report.

TIP SHEET

▶ **The date of publication appears with the title at the top of each report.**

▶ **Report windows may be saved or printed using the Save and Print icons on the Flashbar.**

▶ **To close a report window click on the windows Close button (refer to Chapter 2).**

2 The Consumer Reports window opens with a list box and several icons. The list box contains a collection of reports on automobiles. To review reports specific to Electronics, Home/Workshop, or Money, use the appropriate icon. Use the New icon for the current month's reports.

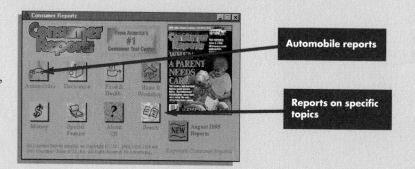

Automobile reports

Reports on specific topics

3 Click on the New icon.

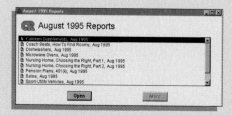

4 The current month's Consumer Reports window opens with a list box displaying this month's reports.

5 Scroll through the list box as necessary to find a report that interests you, select the item, and then click on Open (or double-click on the selected item).

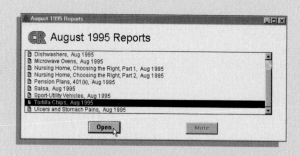

How to Read *National Geographic Online*

The National Geographic Society provides three magazines for you to enjoy online—*National Geographic Magazine*, *National Geographic TRAVELER*, and the children's magazine *National Geographic WORLD*.

In addition, the National Geographic Society provides a wide range of online features and resources including NGS Kids Network, an online Atlas where you can download maps for places all over the world, and educational programs. Everyone in the family will enjoy exploring the world with AOL and the National Geographic Society.

▶ **1** Scroll through the Newsstand list box as necessary and double-click on National Geographic Online. (Or click on the Flashbar's Keyword icon and use the keyword **geographic** or **ngs**.)

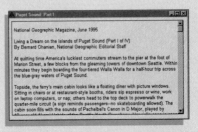

6 Scroll to read the article. If your article has multiple parts like this one, return to step 5 to read each part.

2 The National Geographic Online window opens with a list box displaying National Geographic magazines and icons for National Geographic Society features.

Magazines

Special features

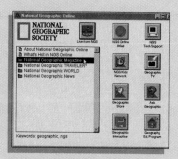

3 Choose the National Geographic Magazine item and double-click.

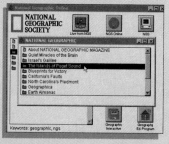

4 The National Geographic window opens displaying a list box of articles. Scroll through the articles to find one that interests you, select the item and double-click.

5 Another window opens, displaying either an article or another list box. If the window displays an article, you can proceed to step 6. If the window displays a list box, scroll as necessary to find an item that interests you, select that item, and then click on Open (or double-click on the list item).

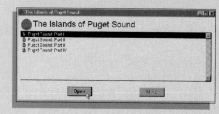

CHAPTER 14

Clubs and Interests

 If you're looking for a place to meet people with common interests, or if you have a hobby or interest you would like more information about, visit AOL's Clubs and Interests department.

The Clubs and Interests department has over 50 clubs and interest groups ranging from business to sports and food to writing. Each club has its own collection of information, message boards, searchable databases, chat rooms and more, all available online.

So get adventurous. Whether you're looking for a new hobby or just trying to find people who share your favorite one, pull up your keyboard and join a club online. It's a great way to meet new friends!

How to Access SeniorNet

If you're 55 or older, and are interested in learning about computers, SeniorNet is just for you. SeniorNet has a Computer Learning Center where you can ask questions about computers or AOL. You can also share your files and projects with other SeniorNet members.

There's more to SeniorNet than just using computers: They also have forums for discussion groups which range from retirement to politics to cooking and grandparenting. If you like meeting new friends online try out the chat area called the Community Center and join in on some of their weekly events and parties.

▶ **1** Make sure you're signed on to AOL and choose Clubs and Interests from the Main menu. (Or click on the Flashbar's Keyword icon and use the keyword **seniornet**.)

7 Return to the SeniorNet Online window in step 4 to explore more areas of SeniorNet.

6 The What's New & Events window opens with a list box of SeniorNet announcements on new services, special events, and online parties. Scroll through the list box as necessary to find an item that interests you, select the item and click on Open (or double-click on the item).

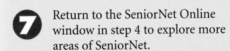

TIP SHEET

▶ **Use the Showcase & Exchange area to find libraries where you can share files (upload or download) with other members.**

▶ **To find information on other senior-related organizations, select Senior Resources from the SeniorNet Online window's list box.**

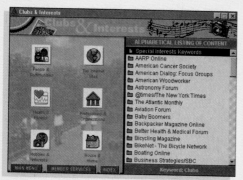

2 The Clubs & Interests window opens with icons and a list box. To find areas listed under general topics, click on the appropriate icon or use the alphabetical listing in the list box.

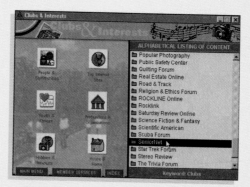

3 Scroll through the list box to find SeniorNet, select the item and double-click.

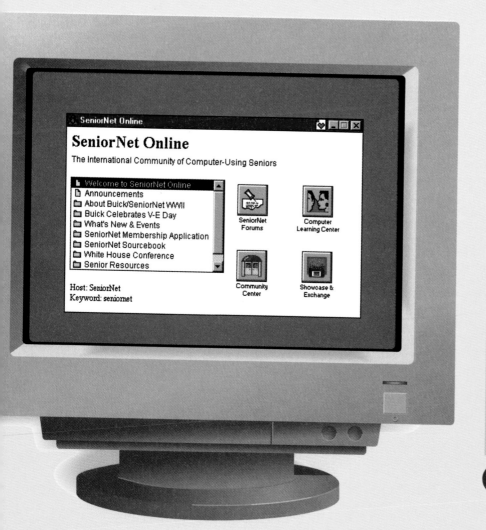

4 The SeniorNet Online window opens. Use the list box to find information on SeniorNet and their activities. Or click on one of the icons to join in a live chat session, message board discussion, or ask questions about your computer. Go ahead, be daring.

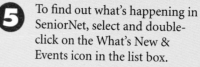

5 To find out what's happening in SeniorNet, select and double-click on the What's New & Events icon in the list box.

How to Get Information about Health and Fitness

AOL's Health & Fitness area covers a broad range of health and fitness topics. The Health and Fitness area includes hundreds of articles by professional health writers, information from organizations and magazines, lists of self-help groups, and more.

So if you're curious about a particular disease, its prevention, diagnosis, or treatment, check AOL's Health & Fitness area.

1 Make sure you're signed on to AOL and choose Clubs and Interests from the Main menu.

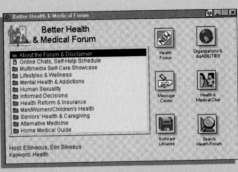

6 The Better Health & Medical Forum window opens. The list box contains topics under which you will find articles on health-related issues. The icons you choose enable you to do many things, including chat with self-help groups and search for information on any topic.

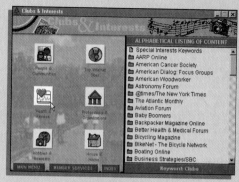

2 The Clubs & Interests window opens with icons and a list box. The list box contains an alphabetical listing of areas, or use the appropriate icon for the topic you're interested in.

3 To find information on Health and Fitness, click on the Health and Fitness icon.

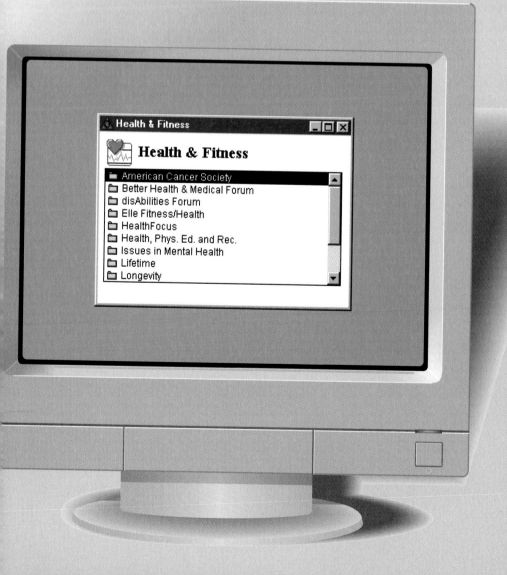

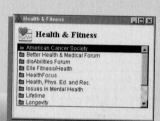

4 The Health & Fitness window opens with a list box of health and fitness areas. Each area covers different health topics and has its own set of features, from message boards to live chat sessions, searchable databases, and even software.

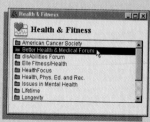

5 To see a wide range of features and topics select and double-click on the Better Health & Medical Forum (or choose an area that has particular interest for you).

How to Visit the Writer's Club

Interested in writing? Join AOL's Writers Club. You'll find information, workshops, and message boards for any type of writing, all online with the Writer's Club.

You can share your writing with other writers in one of many libraries, or download a story or an article that can answer your writing questions. Whether you're interested in fiction, nonfiction, business writing or poetry, there's something for everyone in the Writers Club.

1 Make sure you're signed on to AOL and choose Clubs and Interests from the Main menu.

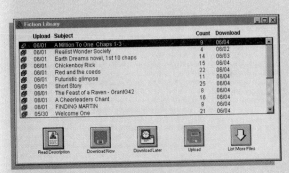

7 The library window opens, listing the files available for downloading. To get a description of a file, select the item and click on Read Description. Once you have found a file that you would like to download, click on either the Download Now or Download Later button (see Chapter 8 for more information on downloading).

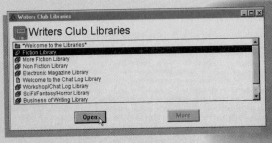

6 The Writers Club Libraries window opens. Scroll through the list box as necessary to find a library that interests you, select the item and click on Open (or double-click on the item).

2 The Clubs & Interests window opens with icons and a list box. The list box contains an alphabetical listing of areas, or use the appropriate icon for the topic you're interested in.

3 Scroll through the list box to find the Writers Club, select the item and double-click. (Or click on the Flashbar's Keyword icon and use the keyword **writers**.)

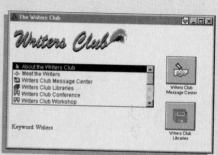

4 The Writers Club window opens. Use the list box to select the writers club area you would like to visit. If you would like to converse with other writers, try the Writers Club Conference or Workshop for live chat sessions.

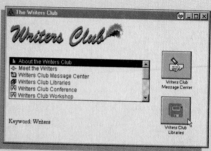

5 To view the libraries in this area click on the Writers Club Libraries icon (or select the Writers Club Libraries item from the list box).

How to Visit the Pet Care Forum

Do you have a question about your pet? Want to meet people who share your interest in a particular animal? AOL's Pet Care Forum is the place to visit.

The Pet Care Forum, sponsored by the Veterinary Information Network, has a staff of veterinarians and animal care experts to provide you with information on animal husbandry and health care topics. Now you can ask questions, read through libraries, and chat with other pet lovers, all online in AOL's Pet Care Forum.

▶ **1** Make sure you're signed on to AOL and choose Clubs and Interests from the Main menu.

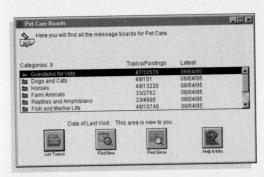

7 A Pet Care Boards window opens, listing the available categories. Scroll to find a category that interests you, click on that category, and then click on List Topics (or double-click on the category.) Refer to Chapter 6 for help on using message boards.

6 The Pet Care Boards window opens. Click on List Categories to see a listing of pet care message boards.

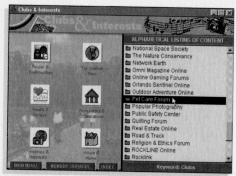

2 The Clubs & Interests window opens with icons and a list box. The list box contains an alphabetical listing of areas, or use the appropriate icon for the topic you're interested in.

3 Scroll through the list box to find the Pet Care Forum, select the item and double-click. (Or click on the Flashbar's Keyword icon and use the keyword **pet care**.)

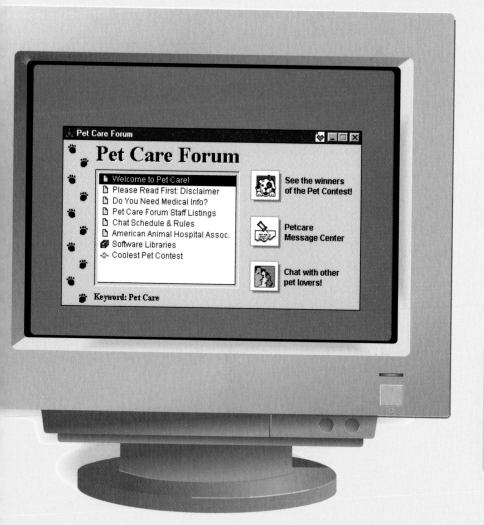

4 The Pet Care Forum window opens. The list box contains information items and access to the Software Libraries. Icons enable you to access the Pet Care Message Center and Chat with other pet lovers.

5 Click on the Pet Care Message Center.

How to Visit the Cooking Forum

If you like to cook, have questions about cooking, or would like to learn about wine, visit the Cooking Forum. You'll see a listing for the Cooking Club, a great place to meet other cooks, share recipes, and pick up tips and information on various aspects of cooking.

If you're looking for a new recipe try The Cookbook, a collection of favorite recipes from families all over the country, or The Celebrity Cookbook with a collection of recipes posted by celebrities.

▶ **1** Make sure you're signed on to AOL and choose Clubs and Interests from the Main menu.

8 Scroll through the article or recipe. To visit more areas in the Cooking Club close the window and return to step 4.

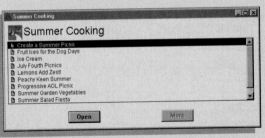

7 A list box opens with articles and recipes. Scroll through the list box to find an item that interests you, select the item and click on Open (or double-click on the selected item).

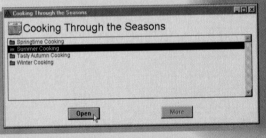

6 The Cooking Through the Seasons window opens. Select an item that interests you and click on Open (or double-click on the item).

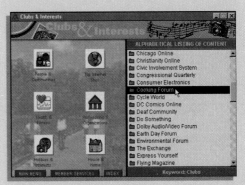

2 The Clubs & Interests window opens with icons and a list box. The list box contains an alphabetical listing of areas, or use the appropriate icon for the topic you're interested in.

3 Scroll through the list box to find the Cooking Forum, select the item and double-click. (Or click on the Flashbar's Keyword icon and use the keyword **cooking**.)

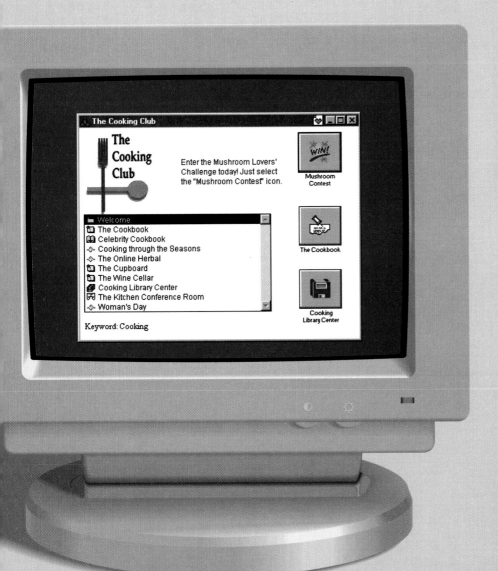

4 The Cooking Club window opens with a list box of Cooking Club areas. The Cooking Club area includes several message boards located in The Cupboard, The Wine Cellar, and The Cookbook. There is also a chat area, the Kitchen Conference Room, where both formal and informal chats are held.

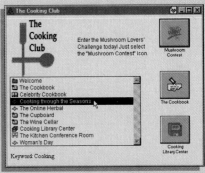

5 Double-click on Cooking Through the Seasons.

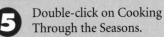

CHAPTER 15

Education

 AOL's Education Department is packed with exciting educational information and resources for students, teachers, and parents, plus a career center to help you find a job once you've finished your education. Resources range from television and radio stations to museums, databases, and even an online university.

Students will find assistance with educational planning and career options, an electronic university, plus software on math, science, languages, art and more!

Teachers' resources include lesson plans, places to gather with other educators and exchange ideas, and information and discussion on important educational issues.

Everyone in the family will enjoy touring exhibits at the Library of Congress and the Smithsonian Online, all without traveling to Washington, D.C. Make learning fun—use the educational resources on AOL!

How to Visit a Television or Radio Station

AOL's Education Department offers access to several television and radio stations. Each of these stations has its own mix of educational programs and activities for the classroom and home.

Now you can track the progress of breaking news and get storyline updates online, plus access databases and transcripts of the station. Or maybe your class would like to take an electronic field trip and experience places, people, and cultures far away from the classroom and your hometown.

Next time you're looking for something exciting in the news, take a tour through one of the television or radio stations online with AOL.

▶ **1** Make sure you're signed on to AOL and click on Education in the Main menu. (Or click on the Flashbar's Keyword icon and use the keyword **education.**)

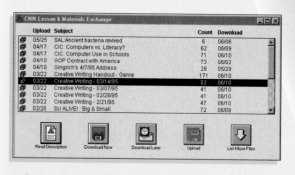

6 A new window opens with a list box containing the available materials in the selected library. Scroll through the list box as necessary to find an item that interests you. Use the Read Description button to find out more information about a particular item. When you are ready to download an item, click on the Download Now button. (Refer to Chapter 8 for more information on downloading files.)

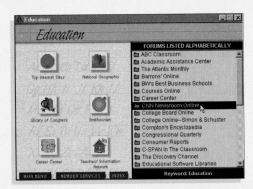

2 The Education window opens. Scroll through the list box as necessary to find the CNN Newsroom Online item, select the item and double-click.

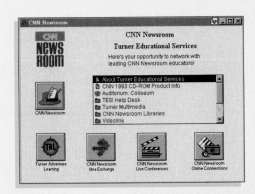

3 The CNN Newsroom window opens. Use the list box to find features in this area. Additional features may be accessed using the icons in this window.

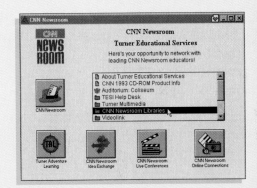

4 Scroll through the list box to find the CNN Newsroom libraries item (or choose an item of interest to you), select the item and double-click.

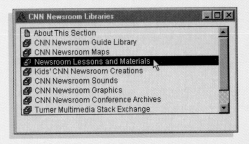

5 The CNN Newsroom Libraries window opens with a list box of the libraries available. Select a library that interests you and double-click.

How to Visit the Library of Congress

Now you can visit the Library of Congress in the comfort of your own home. Each exhibit is as unique as the subject itself, with different areas to explore. New exhibits are being added all the time, so you'll want to visit often.

▶ **1** Make sure you're signed on to AOL and click on Education in the Main menu. (Or click on the Flashbar's Keyword icon and use the keyword **library** and skip to step 3.)

8 Return to step 4 to tour more areas of the library.

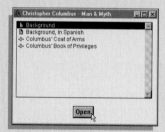

7 Scroll as necessary to read the information window.

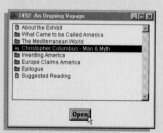

6 Another window opens, displaying either text or another list box. If the window displays text, you can proceed to step 8. If the window displays a list box, scroll as necessary to find an item that interests you, select that item, and then click on Open. Repeat this step as necessary until a text window opens.

TIP SHEET

▶ **Special software is required for viewing graphic files. If you do not have the appropriate viewer on your computer, download the one listed with the exhibit. To download the viewer, select the item and double-click. Another window will open listing the file to be downloaded. Click on Download Now.**

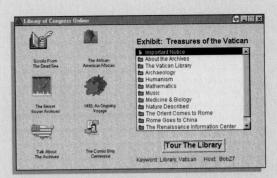

2 The Education window opens, click on the Library of Congress icon.

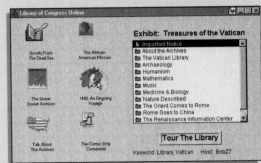

3 The Library of Congress window opens. This window contains a list box and icons for the current exhibits at the library.

4 Click on the 1492: An Ongoing Voyage icon.

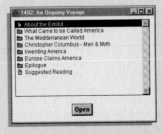

5 The 1492: An Ongoing Voyage window opens. The list box contains different areas of the exhibit to visit. Select Christopher Columbus - Man & Myth (or one that interests you) and click on Open.

How to Get Help for Teachers

A OL's area for teachers, the Teachers' Information Network, is packed with resources, education libraries, forums, and information on professional organizations. Teachers of all disciplines will find information on lesson plans, grants, curriculum ideas, assessment, and technology in the classroom.

There are opportunities to get your students involved in interactive, global learning activities and an online university where you can take live classes.

1 Make sure you're signed on to AOL and click on Education in the Main menu. (Or click on the Flashbar's Keyword icon and use the keyword **tin** and skip to step 3.)

 7 Scroll as necessary to read the text.

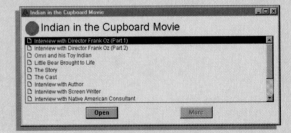

6 Another window opens displaying either text or another list box of items relating to your chosen subject. If text is displayed, proceed to step 8. If the window displays a list box, scroll as necessary to find an item that interests you, select that item, and then click on Open. Repeat this step as necessary until a text window opens.

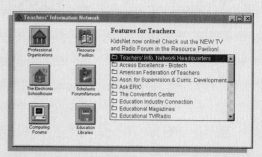

2 The Education window opens. Click on the Teachers' Information Network icon.

3 The Teacher's Information Network opens with a list box and icons displaying the features available for teachers.

4 The Scholastic Forum/Network, one of the many features available in this window, is an online service for K-12 educators and students. To visit this area click on the Scholastic Forum/Network icon.

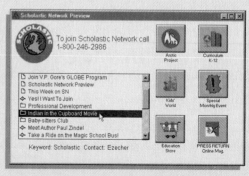

5 The Scholastic Network Preview window opens. Scroll through the list box to find an item that interests you, select the item and double-click.

How to Use the Career Center

Looking for a new job or help with your career? Or maybe you want to find out about trends in the job market so you can plan your education and future.

The Career Center offers a variety of services including a database of job openings, career counseling, and even help with your résumé. Try the Career Center at AOL; your next job may be only keystrokes away.

▶ **1** Make sure you're signed on to AOL and click on Education in the Main menu. (Or click on the Flashbar's Keyword icon and use the keyword **career** and skip to step 3.)

7 Scroll as necessary to read the job announcement. Each announcement will include information about the job opening and how to apply.

6 Scroll through the list box to find a job that interests you, select the item and double-click. (To change your search criterion, return to step 5.)

TIP SHEET

▶ **Help Wanted-USA's database is updated weekly. The database includes two weeks of job listings at any time.**

▶ **The job location is listed by state abbreviation at the end of each item.**

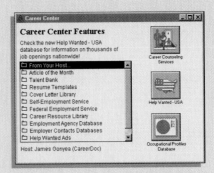

2 The Education window opens. Click on the Career Center icon.

3 The Career Center window opens displaying the features in this area.

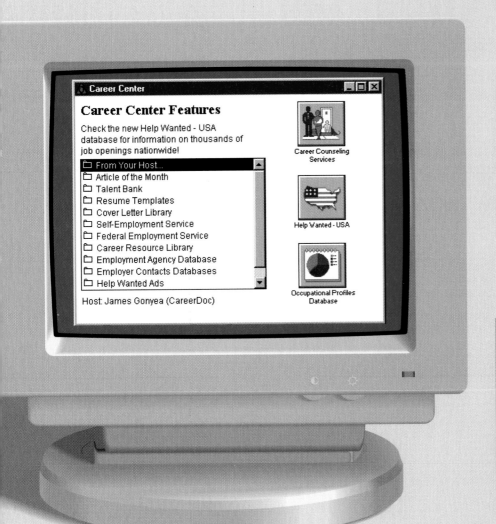

4 To use a searchable database for job hunting, click on the Help Wanted-USA icon.

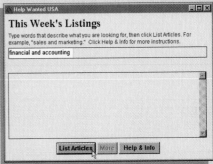

5 To begin your job search, type a search criterion in the text box at the top of the search window, and then click on List Articles. (Refer to Chapter 11 for help on searching.)

CHAPTER 16

Computing

 Want to learn more about CD-ROMs, computer graphics, or software programming? Or maybe you'd just like someone to answer your hardware and software questions, in English? Visit the Computing Department on AOL.

The Computing Department has forums for hardware, operating systems, applications, and more, where computer users—new and advanced—can ask questions and get answers from other members. They also have an area where you can get answers from industry experts!

If you're interested in software, you can learn how to write your own programs in one of AOL's classes or add to your collection by downloading from the thousands of public domain and shareware files available on AOL.

How to Use the Computing Forum

AOL's computing forums cover issues on hardware, software, operating systems, games, and more. Forums provide a mix of information from message boards, software libraries, and technical support from the computer industry and magazines. So if you've got a question, an answer, or a great idea, share it with other AOL members through one of the computing forums.

One forum you may find particularly useful is the Windows forum, which includes a staff of experienced Windows users working to stay up on all of the latest windows tips, tricks, utilities, and software. To learn more about the Windows forum, read on!

1 Make sure you're signed on to AOL and click on Computing in the Main menu. (Or click on the Flashbar's Keyword icon and use the keyword windows forum and skip to step 4.)

8 A window opens with a listing of the message board topics for Windows 95. Select a topic that interests you and click on the List Messages button to begin reading messages (refer to Chapter 6).

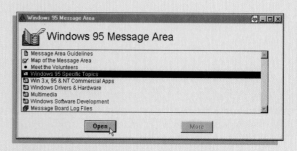

7 You are now in the message board area for Windows 95. Click on the Browse Folders icon to see a list of message boards for Windows 95.

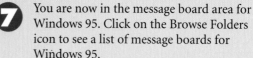

2 The Computing window opens. If the Computing Spotlight window opens in front of the Computing window, click on Go To Computing at the bottom of the window.

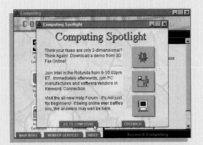

3 The Computing window contains a list box with an alphabetical listing of forums in this area. It also displays several icons to access additional computing areas.

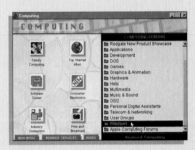

4 Scroll through the list box to find the Windows item you want, select the item and double-click.

5 A Windows Forum window opens. Scroll through the list box to find an interesting item, select the item and double-click.

6 Another window opens with a list box of items, including information and help for this area. Select the Windows 95 Topics item and click on Open.

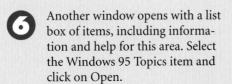

How to Use the Software Center

I f you're confused about all of the software libraries online and how to use them, the Software Center's a great place to start. This area was created so that you can see just what types of utilities and applications are available in the computing forums.

Visit the Software Center to discover programs you never even knew you needed.

▶ **1** Make sure you're signed on to AOL and click on Computing in the Main menu. (Or click on the Flashbar's Keyword icon and use the keyword **software** and skip to step 3.)

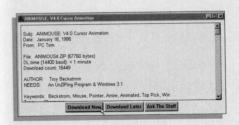

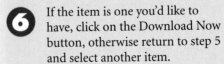

6 If the item is one you'd like to have, click on the Download Now button, otherwise return to step 5 and select another item.

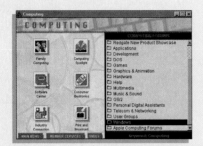

2 The Computing window opens. Click on the Software Center icon.

3 The Software Center window opens. This area, a sampler of what's available in the forum libraries, provides you with an idea of just what types of software are available for downloading.

4 Click on the Software Center Features icon.

5 The Windows Favorites window opens with a listing of windows software. Scroll through the list box for an interesting item, select the item and click on Read Description.

How to Find Windows Shareware

The Windows Shareware 500 Library is located in the Computing Print & Broadcast area—the place to go to find all the latest information on computers. If want to find the top 500 Windows shareware files, they're all available on AOL through this library. This area also has message boards so you can post messages to the author of *The Windows Shareware 500* book.

▶ **1** Make sure you're signed on to AOL and click on Computing in the Main menu. (Or click on the Flashbar's Keyword icon and use the keyword **win500** and skip to step 4.)

6 Another window will open listing the shareware available in this category. Scroll through the list box to find items of interest to you. Use the Read Description button for more information on specific items of shareware.

Use the Download Now button to begin transferring files to your computer.

TIP SHEET

▶ To order the companion book to this library, *The Windows Shareware 500,* click on the Order the Book button in the Windows Shareware 500 window (see step 4). The book reviews and describes the top 500 Windows Shareware files, all of which are available in AOL's Windows Shareware 500 software library.

▶ To see the hottest Windows Shareware software in one listing, click on The Most of the Best button in the Windows Shareware 500 window.

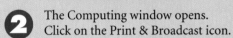

2 The Computing window opens. Click on the Print & Broadcast icon.

3 In the Computing Print & Broadcast window scroll through the list box to find Windows Shareware 500, select the item and double-click.

4 The Windows Shareware 500 window opens. The list box in this window displays the categories for selecting windows software.

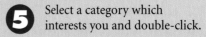

5 Select a category which interests you and double-click.

How to Explore *Windows Magazine*

The *Windows Magazine Online* area is more that just a magazine: It also features a software library, a message exchange, a chat area, a Tips and Tricks area, and you won't want to miss their Web site.

Of course you'll find news, columns, and features from the *Windows Magazine* printed issues. So stop in; this is an area you'll want to visit again and again.

▶ **1** Make sure you're signed on to AOL and click on Computing in the Main menu. (Or click on the Flashbar's Keyword icon and use the keyword **winmag** and skip to step 4.)

7 Use the scroll bars as necessary to read the article.

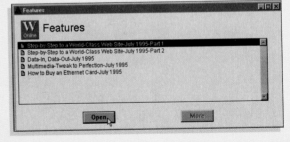

6 Another window opens containing either an article or another list box. If the window contains an article, proceed to step 7. If the window contains a list box, select an item and click on Open. Repeat as necessary until you reach an article window.

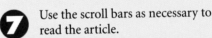

TIP SHEET

▶ **For answers to Frequently Asked Questions, click on the WinMag FAQ icon in the *Windows Magazine* window.**

▶ **Click on the Back Issues icon if you miss an issue of *Windows Magazine*.**

2 The Computing window opens.
Click on the Print and Broadcast icon.

3 Scroll through the list box to find
the *Windows Magazine* item, select
the item, and double-click.

4 The *Windows Magazine* window opens. The list box contains an electronic table of
contents for the magazine.
Windows Magazine also offers
online users several special
features. Use the icons to
access these areas.

5 Scroll through the list
box to find an item that
interests you, select the
item and double-click.

How to Use the Family Computing Forum

The Family Computing Forum is an area where you can learn about computers, meet other members, and learn how to get around and make the most use of AOL. This area is divided into rooms, each with its own special features to make you and your family feel comfortable on your visits.

You'll find discussions on rating video games, news and reviews of computer products, and family games and fun. There's even an album where you can add a picture of your family to share with other AOL families.

1 Make sure you're signed on to AOL and click on Computing in the Main menu. (Or click on the Flashbar's Keyword icon and use the keyword fc and skip to step 3.)

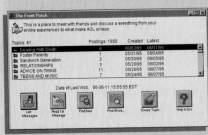

7 Scroll through the list box as necessary to find a topic that interests you, select the item and click on List Messages to peruse the message board or to post a message of your own. (Refer to Chapter 6 for assistance.)

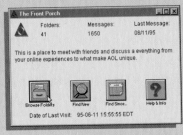

6 The Front Porch window opens. To view the available message boards for this area click on Browse Folders.

2 The Computing window opens. Click on the Family Computing icon.

3 The Family Computing Forum has several special rooms, each with its own features. Each room is accessible by clicking one of the icons in this window.

4 Click on the Family Room icon.

5 To visit the family-oriented message boards in this area, click on The Front Porch.

CHAPTER 17

Reference

The Reference Desk on AOL is much like the one at your local library. Its purpose is to point you to the area with the appropriate resources available to answer your questions, conduct research, and find subject-specific information.

AOL's Reference Desk also provides several areas your local library may not have. For instance, you can access experts at AskERIC, National Geographic, and the Smithsonian Institution through AOL's Reference Desk. Or use the Internet access to "burrow" through the Internet with gopher and WAIS.

Like the reference area in your library, you'll find an encyclopedia. AOL provides *Compton's Encyclopedia* with an added feature—you can access it through a searchable database to make finding information fast and easy!

So the next time you need to find information, use the resources found at AOL's Reference Desk.

How to Use Reference Help

AOL's Reference Help area provides you with access to many services where you can get help finding information. Use the Reference Q&A chat area to ask your research questions and get directions to AOL resources live. Or leave a message on one of the message boards in the Talk About Reference area and get help from other AOL members.

In addition, the Reference Help area gives you access to expert help through the AskERIC Online, Ask National Geographic and Ask the Smithsonian options. So what are you waiting for? With all the help you can get online, finishing that report will be easy.

▶ **1** Make sure you're signed on to AOL and click on Reference Desk in the Main menu. (Or click on the Flashbar's Keyword icon and use the keyword **reference**.)

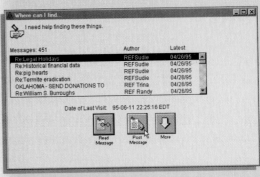

7 To post a message to the board, click on Post Message. (Refer Chapter 6 for help on posting to a message board.)

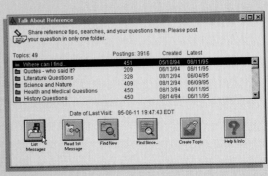

6 A new window opens with a list box of reference topics. Scroll through the list box to find an appropriate message board for your question, select the folder and click on List Messages.

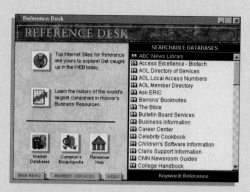

2 The Reference Desk window opens. The list box contains an alphabetical listing of the searchable databases available in this area. The icons in this window provide access to other Reference Desk areas.

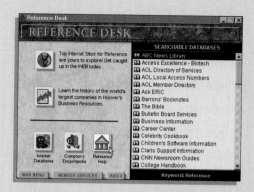

3 To get help in the Reference Desk area, click on the Reference Help icon.

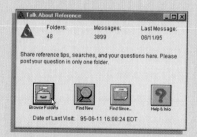

5 The Talk About Reference area gives you access to message boards, which are organized by topic. Click on the Browse Folders icon to find a message board where you can post your question.

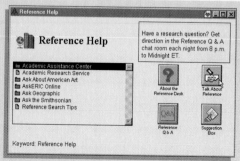

4 The Reference Help window opens. To get help from other AOL members, click on the Talk About Reference icon.

How to Use Compton's Encyclopedia

Compton's Encyclopedia has thousands of articles accessible online. Access to information in *Compton's Encyclopedia* is provided through a searchable database like the ones we discussed in Chapter 11. You can search for encyclopedia articles by their title or on the full text of the document.

▶ ❶ Make sure you're signed on to AOL and click on Reference Desk in the Main menu. (Or click on the Flashbar's Keyword icon and use the keyword **encyclopedia** and skip to step 3.)

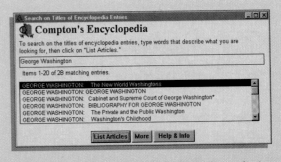

❻ Your search criterion will produce a listing of matching entries. Scroll through the listing to find an article that interests you, select the item and double-click.

2 The Reference Desk window opens, click on *Compton's Encyclopedia.*

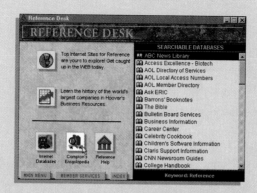

3 The *Compton's Encyclopedia* window opens. The list box contains help information if you need assistance with using the encyclopedia.

4 To search the contents of *Compton's Encyclopedia* by the title of the article, click on Search on Titles.

5 Type your search criterion in the box at the top of the search window, then click on List Articles.

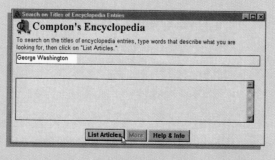

CHAPTER 18

Personal Finance

 If you're looking for investment, financial, and business news from around the world, AOL's Personal Finance department is the place to visit.

Personal Finance gives you access to resources for in-depth analysis of mutual funds, real estate, and stock market investments. Use their searchable database to find company profiles on public and private companies worldwide. Or maybe you're a small business owner: AOL has an area just for small businesses to get support from experts and other small-business owners.

If you're interested in playing the stock market, but you're not quite ready to use your own money, set up a "shadow" portfolio to track your favorite stocks. Once you've decided it's safe to trust your investment intuition, use AOL's online brokerage to set up an account where you can buy and sell for real.

If all these resources are interesting, but you just need a little help with your taxes, don't worry, AOL's got that area covered too. Even the Internal Revenue Service has information online.

How to Read Financial News

The Financial Newsstand makes it easy for you to locate all of your favorite financial magazines. You'll also find business and stock market news from around the world plus economic and company information and reports on the major stock exchanges.

▶ **1** Make sure you're signed on to AOL and click on Personal Finance in the Main menu. (Or click on the Flashbar's Keyword icon and use the keyword **finance**.)

6 Another window opens displaying either stock market information or another list box. If the window displays stock market information, use the scroll bar as necessary to read the information. If the window displays a list box, repeat step 5.

TIP SHEET

▸ **Once you know a particular magazine's keyword, you can use that keyword to bypass the Financial Newsstand window and jump directly to that magazine.**

▸ **To print or save an article use the Flashbar's Print and Save icons.**

2 The Personal Finance window opens. Click on Financial Newsstand.

3 The Financial Newsstand window opens displaying financial news sources. Choose the Market News item and double-click. (Or explore the online publications on your own. If you need help refer to Chapter 13, How to Read an Online Magazine.)

Click here for drop down list box.

4 The Stock Market Details window opens. Click on the down arrow for a drop-down list box and use your mouse pointer to select a category that interests you.

5 Select an item in the list box and click on Open (or double-click on the item).

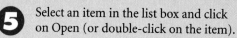

How to Use the Personal Finance Forums

AOL's Personal Finance Forums are set up so that you can discuss a wide range of subjects, from Financial Planning to Investment Software to Taxes, with experts and other AOL members. You'll find message boards, chat rooms, and other information resources to help you with all your financial questions.

1 Make sure you're signed on to AOL and click on Personal Finance in the Main menu. (Or click on the Flashbar's Keyword icon and use the keyword **finance**.)

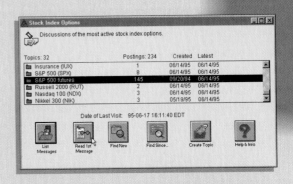

7 Scroll through the list box in the new window to find a topic that interests you, select the topic and click on Read 1st Message to begin reading information on the selected topic.

TIP SHEET

▶ **If you can't find a topic that interests you, create a new topic by clicking on Create Topic in the category window of the message board.**

▶ **Once you have visited a message board, use the Find New and Find Since icons to read only new messages posted since your last visit.**

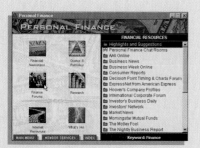

2 The Personal Finance window opens. Click on Finance Forums.

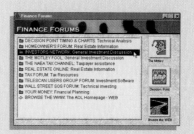

3 The Finance Forums window opens. The list box displays the financial forums available. Select one that interests you and double-click.

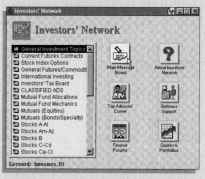

4 Online forum windows are as different as the forums themselves. Each forum has its own special features, in addition to a message board area where you can participate in discussions and exchange information. Click on the Main Message Board icon.

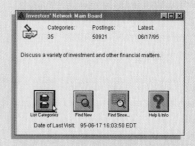

5 Click on the List Categories icon to see the message board categories available.

6 A new window opens listing the available categories. Scroll through the list box to find a category that interests you, select the category and click on List Topics.

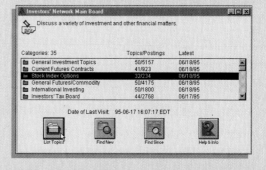

How to Track Stocks and Mutual Funds

Do you own stock, mutual funds, or bonds? Are you interested in seeing how your investments are doing? If so, check out AOL's Quotes and Portfolios. They are updated frequently throughout each business day, and include a wealth of information—from current price to price/earnings (P/E) ratio.

▶**1** Make sure you're signed on to AOL and click on Personal Finance in the Main menu. (Or click on the Flashbar's Quotes & Portfolios icon and skip to step 3.)

9 To look up another stock symbol and get another quote, return to the Search Symbols window, and repeat step 7.

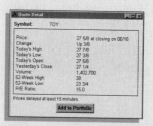

8 A Quote Detail window opens, listing your chosen stock's quote.

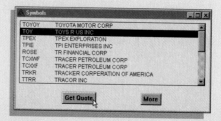

7 The Symbols window opens, listing the companies and their stock symbols that resemble your search criterion. Scroll as necessary, click on the desired stock symbol and company name, and then click on Get Quote. (Or double-click on the stock symbol and company name.) If you can't find your desired symbol and company by scrolling, click on the More button to add more items to the list.

TIP SHEET

▶ Once you've found a stock symbol you need make a note of it. As you can see, knowing the symbol up front can save you quite a few steps.

▶ If you're new to the world of investments and interested in learning more, check out AOL's personal finance area, **Your Money**. To get there, use the keyword *your money*.

▶ The Add to Portfolio button, shown in a number of screens on this page, enables you to set up an online portfolio of stocks just for fun (no real money involved). For more information on creating your own portfolio, click on the Help and Info button in the Quotes & Portfolios window.

▶ You can also buy real stocks with real money, through AOL's TradePlus feature. To access this feature, click on the TradePlus button in the Quotes & Portfolios window.

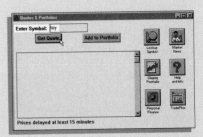

2 The Personal Finance window opens. Click on Quotes & Portfolios.

3 The Quotes & Portfolios window opens, providing a variety of options for retrieving stock information. Every publicly traded stock has a unique stock symbol—an abbreviation of the company's name. If you know it, type the symbol for your desired stock in the Enter Symbol text box, and click on Get Quote. If you don't know the symbol for your stock, skip to step 5.

4 If AOL recognizes your stock symbol, then the window's list box displays that stock's current quote. To get an additional quote, delete your stock symbol from the Enter Symbol text box, and repeat step 3. Otherwise, you can skip the rest of this activity.

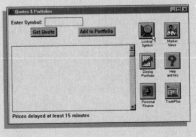

6 The Search Symbols window opens, providing you with two ways to search for stock symbols: by company and by symbol. If you know the company name, type the first few characters of the name into the text box, and then click on Search By Company. If you only know part of the stock symbol, type the first few characters of that symbol in the text box, and then click on Search By Symbol.

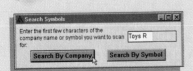

5 To have AOL help you determine a stock symbol, click on Lookup Symbol.

How to Find Personal Finance Software

Would you like to try new financial software, for free? AOL's Personal Finance Software Center offers a wide selection of shareware and public-domain software to monitor your investments, track your expenses, organize your financial plan, and more.

Personal finance software is divided into libraries to help you quickly locate the programs you need. You'll also find software reviews on the most popular programs to help you decide if it's right for you.

Make your life easier, get the software you need to manage your finances, and try it for free!

▶ **1** Make sure you're signed on to AOL and click on Personal Finance in the Main menu. (Or click on the Flashbar's Keyword icon and use the keyword **PFSoftware** and skip to step 3.)

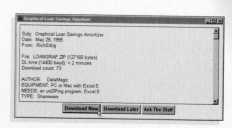

6 Click on Download Now to download the software to your computer.

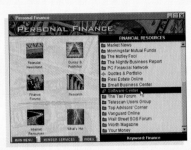

2 The Personal Finance window opens. Scroll through the list box to find the Software Center item, select the item and double-click.

3 The Personal Finance Software Center window opens, and the list box displays the categories of software available. This area also includes an area for uploading new software, software reviews, the editor's best picks of software and more.

4 Scroll as necessary to find a software category that interests you, select the category and double-click.

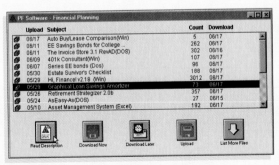

5 A new window will open listing software available for your chosen category. Scroll to find an item that interests you. Select an item you're interested in, then use the Read Description button to get more information about it.

How to Get Help with Your Taxes

A re you ready for tax time? If you've got a question about your federal or state taxes, AOL's a great place to find answers. The Tax Forum on AOL gives you access to tax tips, tax experts, and of course information from the Internal Revenue Service. Plus information on tax software packages. You can't make paying taxes go away, but with a little help from AOL's Tax Forum you can make it less painful.

▶ **1** Make sure you're signed on to AOL and click on Personal Finance in the Main menu. (Or click on the Flashbar's Keyword icon and use the keyword Tax and skip to step 3.)

7 Scroll to read the text.

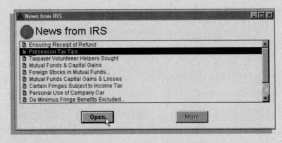

6 Another window opens displaying either text or another list box. If the window displays text, proceed to step 7. If the window displays a list box, scroll as necessary to find an item that interests you, select that item, and then click on Open.

TIP SHEET

▶ **For tax help from the experts use the NAEA TAX CHANNEL icon.**

▶ **For tax tips, try the Ernst and Young Tax Guide. It also includes line-by-line instructions for filling out your tax return.**

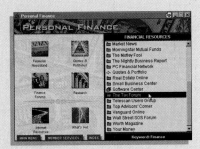

2 Scroll through the list box to find The Tax Forum, select the item and double-click.

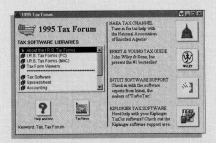

3 This year's Tax Forum window opens. The list box contains an alphabetical listing of the Tax Software Libraries. Or get help with your taxes and tax software by clicking on one of the icons.

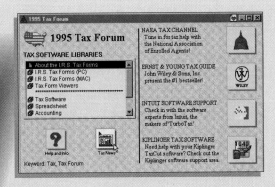

4 Click on Tax News.

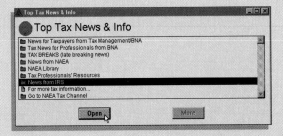

5 A new window opens. Select an item in the list box that interests you and click on Open.

CHAPTER 19

Sports

 On your mark, get set, go! to AOL's Sports area for all the fun and excitement of your favorite sporting events. College, major and minor leagues, team and individual sports—you'll find them all in this area. Plus you can yell, scream, argue, and cheer with other sports fans just like yourself.

You'll find sports highlights and all the latest happenings on and off the courts, fields, tracks, rinks, and rings. And of course, up-to-date scores and news from the world of sports.

If you get tired of watching, how about participating? Try your skills in one of the simulation leagues from golf to baseball to auto racing (yes, auto racing).

So put on your favorite jersey, it's time to play ball!

How to Read Sports News

Sports News provides you with the latest scores, game recaps, injury reports, and more. Use the sports news area to get a quick update on the latest events in the sports world day and night.

If you missed an inning, quarter, match, or lap, sports news will bring you up-to-date.

▶ **1** Make sure you're signed on to AOL and click on Sports in the Main menu. (Or click on the Flashbar's Keyword icon, use the keyword **Sports News** and skip to step 3.)

7 Scroll to read the text.

6 Another window opens, displaying either text or a list box. If the window displays text, proceed to step 7. If the window displays a list box, scroll as necessary to find an item that interests you, select that item, and then click on Open.

TIP SHEET

▶ If you just need the latest scores, click on the Scoreboard icon and select the appropriate sport. You will see a listing of games; click on the team item for scores.

▶ To find more information on a specific team or athlete, click on the Search News icon. (Refer to Chapter 11 for details.)

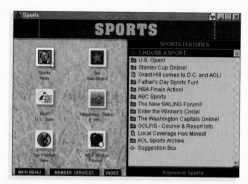

2 The Sports window opens. Click on the Sports News icon.

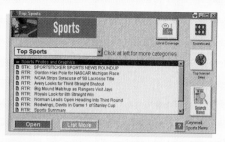

3 Another Sports window opens. Sports categories are listed in the pull-down list box. The articles in the windows list box will change each time you select a new category.

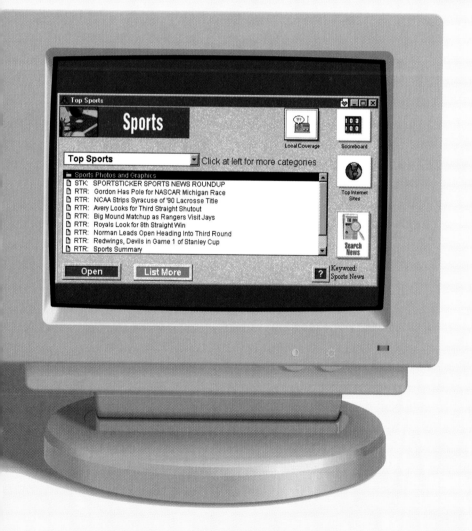

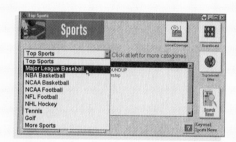

4 Click on the down arrow to open the pull-down list, use your mouse button to select a category, and click once.

5 Scroll as necessary to find an item in the list box that interests you, select the item and click on Open. (If the More button is active, you can use this button to add more items to the list box.)

How to Talk to Other Sports Fans

The Grandstand area is a great place to meet and talk with other sports fans. You'll find message boards, chat rooms, and even interactive conferences in this area.

The chat area, Sports Rooms, and the message board area, Sports Boards, are easily accessible by icons in The Grandstand window. Each sport listed in The Grandstand window also has more sports activities and information available in its own area.

▶ **1** Make sure you're signed on to AOL and click on Sports in the Main menu. (Or click on the Flashbar's Keyword icon, use the keyword **grandstand** and skip to step 3.)

TIP SHEET

▶ **Check the Conference Schedule listed under Sports Rooms for a listing of conference times and locations.**

▶ **Each sport area has a forum leader for you to contact, if you have questions. You can find out who your forum leader is by clicking on the question mark (?) icon in each area.**

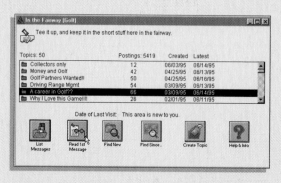

6 Scroll through the list box as necessary to find a topic that interests you. Click on Read 1st Message to begin reading messages.

2 The Sports window opens. Click on The Grandstand.

3 The Grandstand window opens. Scroll through the list box as necessary to find a sport that interests you, select the item and double-click.

4 A new window will open with a list of features available for the sport area you chose. To join in discussions with other sports fans, select the message board area (an item with a pushpin icon).

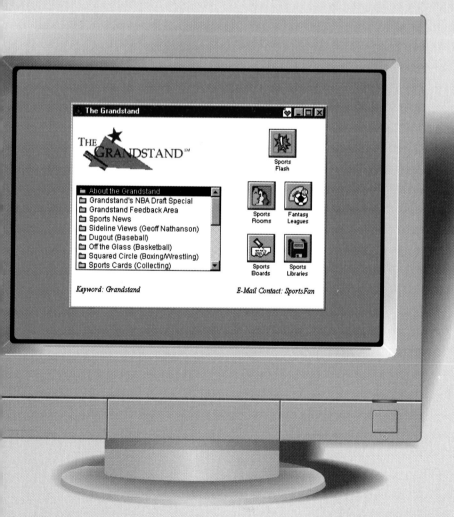

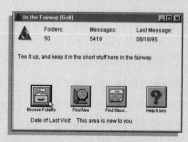

5 Click on the Browse Folders icon to get a list of categories for this message board (refer to Chapter 6).

How to Visit the ABC World of Sports

You've watched ABC Sports on television, now you can visit it on AOL. ABC's World of Sports area is packed with sports highlights, press releases, programming and sporting schedules. You'll also find pictures and video clips, sports message boards, and of course the latest news on the play-offs.

ABC even has a concessions area where you can get a play-off's T-shirt even if you couldn't make the final game.

1 Make sure you're signed on to AOL and click on Sports in the Main menu. (Or click on the Flashbar's Keyword icon, use the keyword **ABC Sports** and skip to step 3.)

7 Scroll to read the text.

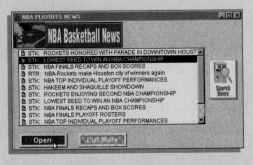

6 Another window opens, displaying either text or another list box. If the window displays text, proceed to step 7. If the window displays a list box, scroll as necessary to find an item that interests you, select that item, and then click on Open.

TIP SHEET

▶ **For press releases, programming and sports schedules, click on Inside ABC Sports.**

▶ **Items in the Sports Concessions area are listed with descriptions. To see a picture of an item before you decide to buy it, use the Product Photo Download library located in the Sports Concessions list box; each item is listed individually.**

2 The Sports window opens. Select ABC Sports in the list box and double-click.

3 The ABC Sports window opens. This area has many features for sports lovers. For this activity, click on SportsBoard (or click on one of the other icons and do some exploring on your own).

4 The SportsBoard window opens. Scroll through the list box to find a sport which interests you and double-click.

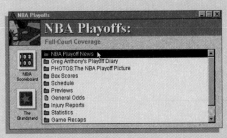

5 Another window opens with a list box of topics for you to explore. Scroll through the list box to find one that interests you, select the item and double-click.

CHAPTER 20

Entertainment

 AOL's Entertainment department has areas for everyone in the family. You'll find everything from motion pictures to cartoons to MTV. And it's not just information and news, there are sound and video clips, pictures, contests, promotions, and more.

Because AOL has so much to offer in the Entertainment department, and because the range of features expands constantly, we can't expect to cover all or even most of them in one chapter. So we'll do our best to introduce you to four exciting features: the motion picture area Hollywood Online, the Critics Choice area where you'll find reviews on all types of entertainment, the music lovers area called MusicSpace, and an area designed for everyone who loves to play games.

These features alone will keep your family busy for hours, and when you're ready you'll find even more entertainment areas to explore online.

How to Access Hollywood Online

I f you're a movie fan you'll enjoy the many features in AOL's Hollywood Online area. This area offers you a look at the latest movies before you go see them at the theater, plus sneak previews of the hottest new pictures. Once you've enjoyed the movie, visit the Picture and Sounds library where you can download pictures of your favorite stars.

Next, join other motion picture enthusiasts and talk about movies on the Movie Talk message boards. AOL members also have chances to receive great promotion items like posters, movie passes, and more. Let's all go to the movies!

1 Make sure you're signed on to AOL and click on Entertainment in the Main menu. (Or click on the Flashbar's Keyword icon, use the keyword **Hollywood** and skip to step 4.)

TIP SHEET

▸ **Once you've read the Sneak Peek Notes, if you'd like to download a video clip or picture, return to step 5, select Sneak Peeks and click on Open. A Previews window will open with a listing of files available for downloading.**

▸ **If you download pictures and video clips you'll need special software to view the files. Double-click on Viewing Tools in the Hollywood Online list box, then select the appropriate list box item for the type of tool you need.**

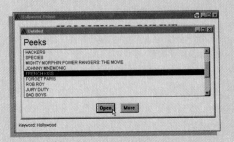

7 Scroll through the Peeks window to find a movie title that interests you. Select the item and click on Open to find out who's starring in the movie, the plot, and more.

2 The Entertainment window opens. The list box has an alphabetical listing of the features available in this area in addition to the areas accessible by icons.

3 Scroll through the list box to find the Hollywood Online item, select the item and double-click.

4 The Hollywood Online window opens. Hollywood Online has areas where you'll find information on movies, movie and sound clips, a place to meet your favorite stars, and more.

5 To get a sneak peek at new movies, scroll through the list box to find the Sneak Peeks item, select the item and double-click.

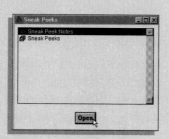

6 The Sneak Peeks window opens. Select Sneak Peek Notes and click on Open to find out more information on new movies.

How to Find Book Reviews and Bestseller Lists

Are you tired of spending money on books and magazines that just don't live up to your expectations? Visit the Critics' Choice area on AOL. Their job is to help you choose the best entertainment for you and your family.

Critics' Choice covers more than books. They've got critics for movies, video, television, music, and games. There's also an area where you can join in the discussions.

For this activity we'll explore how to find book reviews and bestseller lists, then you can try the other areas on your own.

► **1** Make sure you're signed on to AOL and click on Entertainment in the Main menu. (Or click on the Flashbar's Keyword icon, use the keyword **Critics** and skip to step 3.)

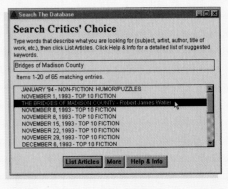

7 Scroll through the list of matching entries to find an item that interests you, select the item and double-click to read the text.

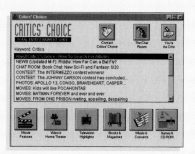

2 The Entertainment window opens. Scroll through the list box to find the Critics' Choice item, select the item and double-click.

3 The Critics' Choice window opens. Use the icons to find critics on the area you're interested in.

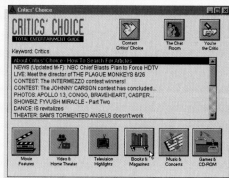

4 Click on the Books and Magazines icon.

5 The Books & Magazines window opens. This window has a list box where you can find book reviews and bestseller lists and a searchable database to help you locate information on a specific book or magazine. Click the Search Critics' Choice icon.

6 Type your search criterion in the text box at the top of the search window, and then click on List Articles. (Refer to Chapter 11 for help on selecting a search criterion).

How to Enjoy Music on America Online

MusicSpace, AOL's music area, is a must for music lovers. You'll find your favorite artists from Alternative to Country, Rock to Rhythm and Blues, and more.

Get the latest tour dates, CD information, and industry happenings all at your fingertips. You'll even find artist profiles, and video and sound clips. If you've just got to keep up with the beat, visit MusicSpace.

▶ **1** Make sure you're signed on to AOL and click on Entertainment in the Main menu. (Or click on the Flashbar's Keyword icon, use the keyword **MusicSpace** and skip to step 3.)

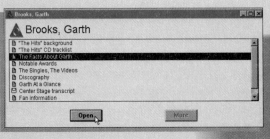

6 Another window opens with a listing of items for the artist you selected. Scroll through the list box to find an item that interests you, select the item and click on Open.

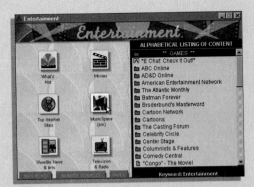

2 The Entertainment window opens. Click on the Music Space icon.

3 MusicSpace has information on your favorite artists as well as sound clips from some of their songs. The list box contains the categories of music under which you'll find artist information.

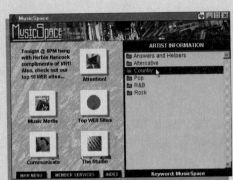

4 Select a music category and double-click.

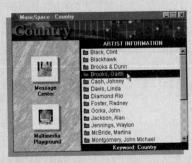

5 The music category window opens. Use the list box to find an artist you're interested in, select the artist and double-click.

How to Find Out about Online Games

K ids and adults need more than school and work; they need to have fun playing games. AOL knows this, and has dozens of different games that you can play online. Most of these games are parlor games (games that you play in a chat room with other AOL members). AOL's parlor games include word games, number games, music games, and trivia games. Some games even offer free online time as prizes. We can't possibly show you how to play all these games on one page, but we will show you where to go to find out more about the games that interest you most.

▶ **1** (Or Click on the Flashbar's Keyword icon, and use the keyword **parlor.**

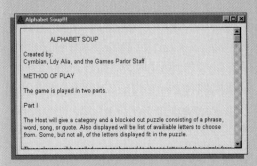

7 Scroll to read text.

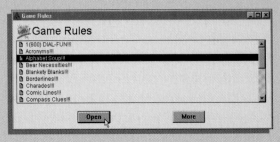

6 To learn the rules of a particular game before you play, return to the Games Parlor window in step 2, and click on the Game Rules icon. A Games Rules window such as this one opens, displaying a partial list of games. If you see the game you want, click on Open.

TIP SHEET

▶ **For kids, if your parents have set up Parental Controls for you, you may not be able to play any online games. Try to convince them that the games are educational (they are!), and to remove these controls for at least a little while.**

▶ **The Entertainment department also has other games, including Neverwinter Nights, a role-playing adventure game, and RabbitJack's Casino, a gambling casino featuring poker, blackjack, and more. Unlike parlor games, though, these games require that you first obtain and set up special game software.**

▶ **Besides online games, you can download any one of AOL's thousands of offline games—games you can play without being signed on. For details on downloading games, see Chapter 8.**

2 The AOL Game Forums window opens. Select the Games Parlor item in the list box and double-click.

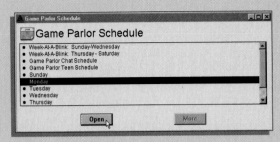

3 The Games Parlor window opens. Click on the Game Schedule icon.

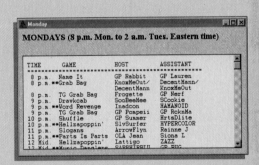

4 The Games Parlor Schedule window opens. Click on the day or the Week-AT-A-Blink set of days that you're available to play online games, and then click on Open.

5 A window opens to show you the People Connection games scheduled for the day or days you chose. Scroll through this window, making notes about the games that sound interesting, and when and where they'll take place. (If you're interested in a lot of games, you can save or print the schedule instead.) Then you can sign on and visit these chat rooms at the scheduled times. (Chapter 10 shows you how to visit chat rooms.)

CHAPTER 21

For Parents Only

 For many families these days, the home computer is a multi-purpose tool. Mom and Dad use it for tracking the family budget and calculating income taxes, the kids spend their computer time doing homework and playing games, and everyone uses the computer to type up personal letters.

As an extension of your computer, AOL also serves a variety of family purposes. Some AOL features, such as stock quotes and airline reservations, appeal primarily to adults. Other features, such as homework help and games, are geared more toward kids. And many features can be equally enjoyed by all, such as e-mail and online magazines. The next two chapters focus on ways to use AOL as a shared family resource.

This chapter is a guide for parents who want to introduce their family to AOL. It shows parents how to share a single AOL membership account among family members, and how to control kids' access to certain AOL areas. Chapter 22 takes a closer look at a selection of AOL features that your kids might want to check out.

How to Share an AOL Account with Your Family

There are several ways you *could* share your AOL account with your family. You could let them use your existing screen name and password, but then any one of them could receive (and even accidentally delete!) your mail, send out messages bearing your name, and so on. You could also get a separate membership account for each family member, but the combined monthly membership fees could really add up. The best way to share your existing AOL membership account is by establishing up to four *subaccounts*—each with a unique screen name and password—under your single account, and still pay the same monthly membership fee. This page shows you how.

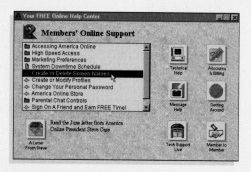

1 Before signing on to AOL, ask each family member to provide a list of suggested screen names for his or her subaccount. Like your own screen name, your family's screen names can be 3 to 10 characters long, including spaces. Because each screen name must be unique to AOL, explain to your family that they may not be able to get exactly the screen names they want. Then, sign on to AOL, open Your FREE Online Help Center (see Chapter 5 for details), and double-click on Create or Delete Screen Names in the window's list box.

Click here for a list of screen names.

8 To sign on to AOL with one of the new screen names, open the Screen Name drop-down list box in either the Welcome window or the Goodbye from America Online! window, click on the desired screen name, type the appropriate password in the Password text box, and then click on Sign On.

 Repeat steps 2–6 for each additional screen name, and then sign off.

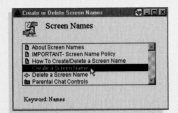

2 The Create or Delete Screen Names window opens. Double-click on Create a Screen Name.

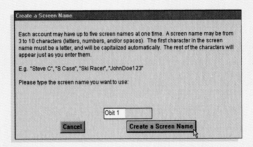

3 The Create a Screen Name dialog box opens. In the text box near the bottom of the window, type a screen name for the first subaccount, and then click on Create a Screen Name.

4 If the screen name you typed in step 3 is unique to AOL, then the Set Password dialog box shown in step 5 opens. Otherwise, AOL will ask you to try other screen names until you either provide a unique screen name or accept one that AOL suggests. (The screen name that AOL suggests is usually a variation of the name you typed, followed by a string of numbers.)

Type the *same* password in both boxes.

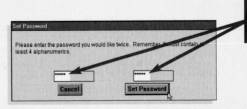

6 If all is well, a dialog box opens to inform you that the screen name has been added to your account. Click on OK to close this dialog box.

5 Type a password for the new screen name in each of the two text boxes. Like your own screen name's password, this password can be 4 to 8 characters long, and should be something that's easily remembered but not easily guessed. (To be safe, write down the password.) For security reasons, the password will display on screen as asterisks. When you're done, click on Set Password.

How to Set Up Parental Chat Controls

Once you've explored AOL's areas, you'll realize that AOL can be a valuable part of your children's education. As in any community, though, AOL's electronic community may provide learning opportunities that you don't want your kids to experience. One of these is the use of foul, abusive, or suggestive language in unmonitored chat rooms or in Instant Messages. Although AOL expressly forbids profanity, it does sometimes occur. If this concerns you, you may want to set up parental chat controls on any or all of your children's sub-accounts to prevent them from visiting certain chat rooms and/or receiving Instant Messages. Here's how.

TIP SHEET

▶ Although parental controls can prevent your kids from using features that are especially prone to member abuse, these controls are not a panacea. Also, they can interfere with some appropriately educational AOL features (see Chapter 22). The best way to help your kids enjoy AOL in the most productive way is to monitor their online sessions.

▶ As an alternative to parental controls, you might want to guide your kids to rooms that are carefully monitored by AOL staff or volunteers, such as Kool Tree House or People Connection's Teen Chat room.

▶ If you or your family do encounter inappropriate language or any other terms-of-service violations in a People Connection chat room, use the keyword *guide pager* and click on the appropriate area button; an AOL representative will assist you. To report violations in other areas, use the keyword *tos*, and then click on Write to Terms of Service Staff. Include as many details as possible, including where you encountered the violation and the offender's screen name.

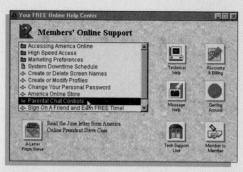

 1 Sign on to AOL using the master account, open Your FREE Online Help Center (see Chapter 5 for details), scroll down in the window's list box, and double-click on Parental Chat Controls. (You may also access Parental Chat Controls by choosing Parental Control in the Members menu, but access through Your FREE Online Help Center is free; access through the Members menu is not.)

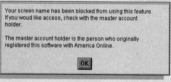

8 Should a family member attempt to use a feature that you've blocked from his or her account, this dialog box will say that the feature is blocked.

 7 A dialog box informs you that your controls have been saved. Click on OK to close this dialog box.

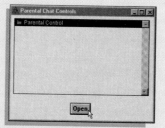

2 The Parental Chat Controls window opens. Click on Parental Control (if necessary), and then click on Open.

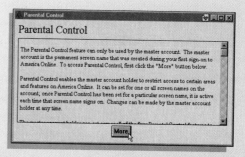

3 A Parental Control window opens, describing how to set parental controls. Read this information if you'd like, and then click on More.

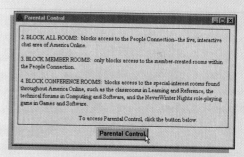

4 A second Parental Control window opens, displaying more information about parental controls. Read this information if you'd like, and then click on Parental Control.

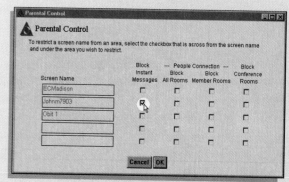

5 A third (and final!) Parental Control window opens, displaying every screen name on your account. To set controls on any or all of these subaccounts, check the corresponding check boxes as needed. Block Instant Messages prevents the receipt or sending of Instant Messages; Block All Rooms prevents entrance to *any* People Connection chat room; Block Member Rooms prevents entrance to any member-created People Connection chat room; and Block Conference Rooms prevents entrance to any chat room *outside* the People Connection department.

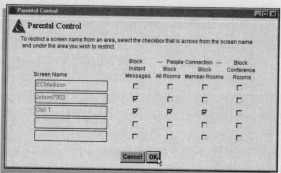

6 Once you've checked all the desired controls, click on OK.

CHAPTER 22

Kids Only

 After a few sessions online you'll realize that AOL offers dozens of educational and entertainment opportunities for kids. These include features designed specifically for youngsters, such as Kids Only message boards and the Teen Chat room, as well as features that can be enjoyed by both kids and adults, such as the Career Center and online games.

Because AOL has so much to offer to young people, and because the range of features expands almost constantly, we can't expect to cover all or even most of them in one chapter. So we'll do our best to introduce you to AOL's most responsive educational feature, the Teacher Pager. We'll also explore the Children's Software Library and a magazine designed and created for kids called *Tomorrow's Morning*.

Note: Except for this introductory page, this chapter is addressed primarily to the kids who will actually be performing the steps shown. If your family is new to AOL, you'll want to familiarize yourself with the next few pages, and then help your kids work through the steps, providing explanations where appropriate.

How to Use the Teacher Pager

Homework can be a real chore. Sometimes the assignment seems boring; other times it's hard to understand. You could ask your parents for help, but you may have found that they don't always know the answers. So who else can you ask for help? Well, who better to help you with homework than a teacher? Through AOL's Teacher Pager, you can ask a teacher questions and get e-mail responses in 3 to 5 hours. Whether the subject is arithmetic or astronomy, zoology or Zagreb, one of AOL's knowledgeable online teachers can guide you toward solving all your homework problems.

1 Make sure you're signed on to AOL and click on Kids Only in the Main menu. (Or click on the Flashbar's Keyword icon, use the keyword **teacher pager** and skip to step 5.)

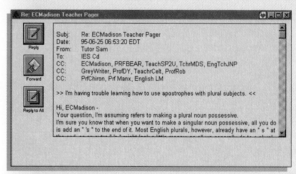

7 Within a few hours you'll receive an e-mail message from one of AOL's teachers with an answer to your question.

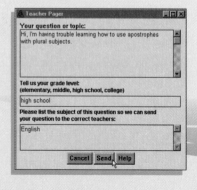

6 A second Teacher Pager window opens. In the window's top text box, describe your homework problem in as much detail as possible. In the second text box, type in your grade level by school type (elementary, middle, high school, college). In the bottom text box type in the subject to help the coordinator decide which teachers will best be able to answer your question. Finally, click on Send, and then click on OK to close the next dialog box.

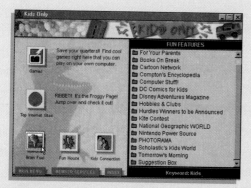

2 The Kids Only window opens. Click on the Brain Fuel icon.

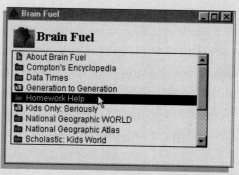

3 The Brain Fuel window opens. Scroll through the list box as necessary to find Homework Help, select the item and double-click.

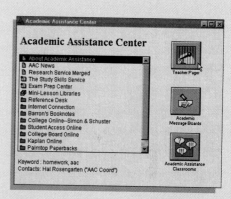

4 An Academic Assistance Center window opens. Click on Teacher Pager.

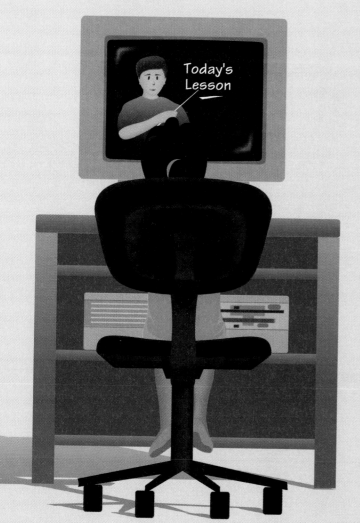

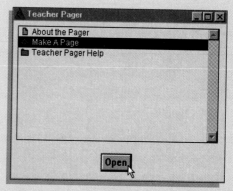

5 A Teacher Pager window opens. Select Make A Page and then click on Open.

How to Use the Children's Software Library

AOL knows that everyone has different interests in computer software and information, so they've created software libraries just for kids. Not only will you find educational software, the Kids Only software libraries include games, puzzles, and guides for writing and programming. Plus a Graphics Library where you can share your art with others.

Show off your talents and share your files with other AOL kids.

▶ 1 Make sure you're signed on to AOL and click on Kids Only in the Main menu. (Or click on the Flashbar's Keyword icon, and use the keyword **kids**.)

8 When you're done using AOL, sign off without exiting AOL for windows. (Choose Exit from the File menu, and then click on Yes.) If the file you downloaded ends with .ZIP or .ARC—indicating that the file is stored in a compressed format to save download time—your AOL software will automatically decompress the file.

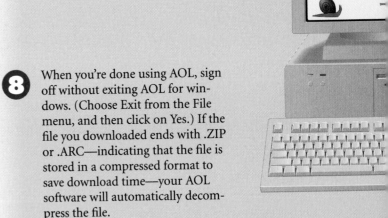

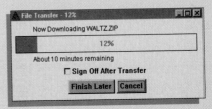

7 A File Transfer dialog box opens, displaying the progress of your file transfer (download). When the download is complete, a Download Manager dialog box opens to indicate this. Click on OK to close the dialog box.

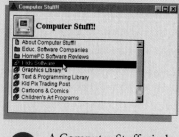

2 The Kids Only window opens. Find the Computer Stuff item in the window's list box and double-click.

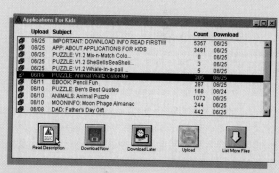

3 A Computer Stuff window opens. Double-click on Kids Software in the window's list box. (Or choose one of the other software libraries for kids— all of the software library items are easily identified by the disk icon.)

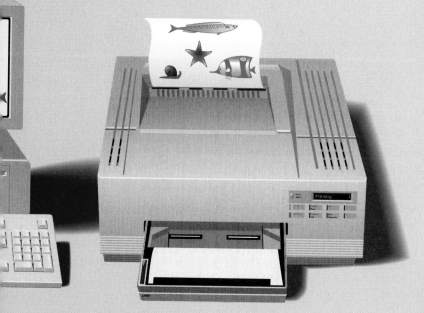

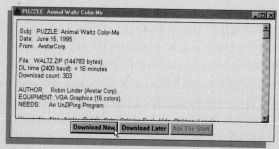

4 The software library window opens. Use the scroll box to find an item that interests you, click on the item with your mouse, then click on Read Description.

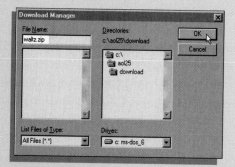

6 A Download Manager window opens, giving you the option to specify a different file name or disk location for the file. For now, just click on OK.

5 A description window for your selected file opens. Read the description carefully. Pay close attention to the estimated time it will take to download the file, the computer equipment and/or software necessary to use the file, and the general description. If you want to download this file, click on Download Now. Otherwise, return to the software library window in step 4.

How to Read and Contribute to *Tomorrow's Morning*

E xtra! Extra! Read *Tomorrow's Morning*, a weekly newspaper designed and created just for kids. The paper covers interesting people, places, and events nationally and around the world in a manner easy for kids to understand and relate to.

Tomorrow's Morning also gives kids a chance to submit an article for publication in online and printed editions; read on and we'll show you how.

▶ **1** Go to the Kids Only area using the icon in the Main menu or the keyword **kids**. Scroll through the Kids Only list box to find the *Tomorrow's Morning* item and double-click.

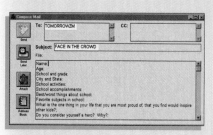

9 The FACE IN THE CROWD QUESTIONNAIRE is now pasted into your compose mail window. Remember to add your addressee in the To: text box and add your subject in the Subject: text box. Then fill out the questionnaire, and click on Send.

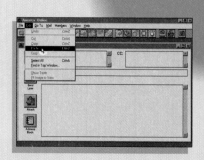

8 Once your compose window is open, click on the message text area, and then click on the Edit menu and select Paste.

7 Then click on the Flashbar's Compose icon. This will open a compose window.

2 The *Tomorrow's Morning* window opens. The list box contains an electronic table of contents for this week's issue of the newspaper. Scroll through the list box to find an item that interests you and double-click.

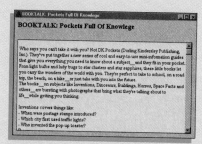

3 An article window opens. Scroll as necessary to read the article. If you would like to find out how you can submit an article to *Tomorrow's Morning* proceed to step 4, otherwise you have completed this activity.

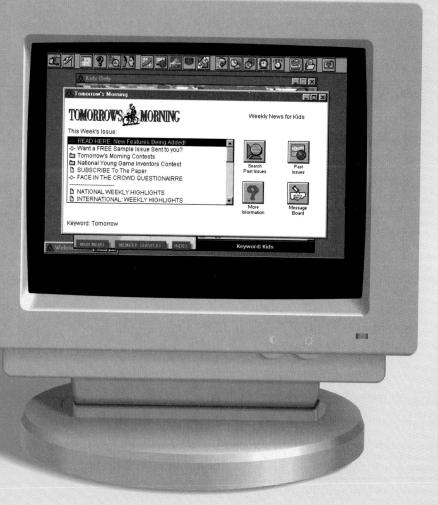

4 To submit an article to *Tomorrow's Morning* Faces in the Crowd area, double-click on the FACE IN THE CROWD QUESTIONNAIRE item in the list box.

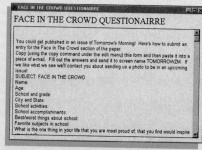

5 The FACE IN THE CROWD QUESTION-NAIRE window opens. You'll need to copy this questionnaire to a compose mail window(don't worry, we'll show you how), complete the form and then mail it to the address identified in the first paragraph.

6 Use your mouse to select the text in the questionnaire, then click on the Edit menu, and select Copy. (This will copy the questionnaire to your clipboard area.)

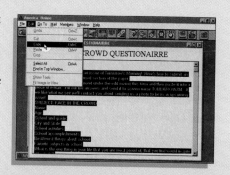

CHAPTER 23

People Connection

 We mentioned the People Connection department in Chapter 10 when we introduced chatting. People Connection is a great place to meet new and old friends.

You'll find not only member chat rooms where you can discuss a wide range of topics in small groups. You'll also find regularly scheduled events in the Center Stage area, where large groups meet to discuss important issues of the day and exchange ideas with AOL's special guests, live of course.

If you miss a Center Stage event don't worry, you can get a transcript of the event and then join the message board discussions with others who were there.

You'll also want to take a tour of AOL's Gallery where you share photographs of yourself and your family with all your new friends.

Day or night visit AOL's People Connection department and join in on what's sure to be a lively discussion of your favorite subject.

How to View Members' Photographs Online

H ave you ever wondered about the face behind the screen name? And how are they
visualizing what you look like? AOL's created
The Gallery just so members can get to know
each other better and put a face to that myste-
rious screen name.

You can also show off your family or that
special group picture you took at the last AOL
member party in the Galleries Family Album
area.

▶ **1** Make sure you're signed on to AOL and
click on People Connection in the Main
menu. (Or click on the Flashbar's People
Connection icon.)

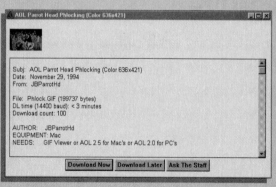

7 The description window opens with a sample of
the photograph you can download and information
on the person or group in the photograph. If you
would like to download this photograph, click on
the Download Now button and follow the download procedures detailed in Chapter 8.

TIP SHEET

▶ **You don't need a scanner to get your
picture online; AOL will scan your
photo and upload it free. Click on
Get Framed in The Gallery's list box
for information on how to submit
your photograph.**

▶ **If you have questions in The Gallery
area click on Frequently Asked
Questions.**

▶ **If you'd like to see what a host or
hostess looks like click on Rogues
Gallery. If your host's portrait isn't
there, encourage him or her to
send it in.**

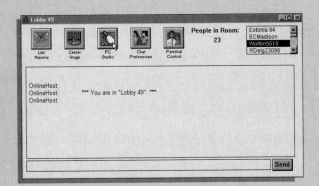

2 A Lobby window opens. Click on PC Studio.

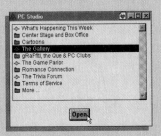

3 The PC Studio window opens. Click on The Gallery.

4 The Gallery window opens with a list box of Gallery's Software libraries where members' photographs are stored. There is also a Family Album item in this list box which contains pictures of members' families and AOL parties. Scroll through the list box to find the Family Album item, select the item and double-click.

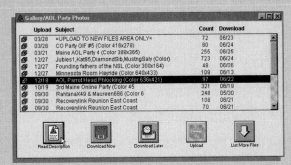

6 A new window opens with a listing of the photographs in this area. Scroll through the box to find an item that interests you, select the item and click on Read Description.

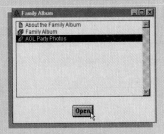

5 The Family Album window opens. Select AOL Party Photos and click on Open.

How to Find Out about Upcoming Events

A s you explore AOL's public chat rooms, you may find it hard to determine the purpose of certain rooms. If you visit the Great Outdoors room, for example, you may only find a few people chatting, and they may be discussing anything *but* the Great Outdoors. This is because many of AOL's public rooms, much like hotel conference rooms, are event-oriented. Visit a hotel conference room between events, and the room seems purposeless; the same is true of AOL's public rooms. This page shows some ways to find out about AOL's *online events*.

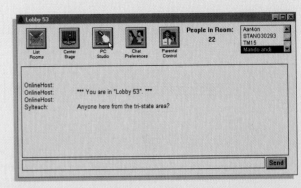

1 Go to the Lobby or to any other People Connection chat room, and then click on PC Studio.

TIP SHEET

▶ The options we've shown you here generally provide information only on regularly scheduled, general-interest events in the People Connection department. To learn about events in other departments, use the keyword tilf.

▶ The Welcome! window that opens when you sign on to AOL, and the Goodbye From America Online! window that opens when you sign off without exiting AOL for Windows often display advertisements for current or upcoming events.

▶ Because of their overwhelming popularity, some events are held in special rooms called *auditoriums*, which are capable of holding more than 23 people at one time. These auditoriums are in the Center Stage area (keyword center stage). Visit the Center Stage Box Office/Coming Attractions area to find out about more upcoming events.

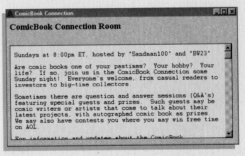

8 A new window opens, containing a description of your chosen event.

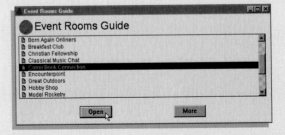

7 An Event Rooms Guide window opens, listing events in alphabetical order. Scroll to find the desired event (using the More button as necessary), click on that event, and then click on Open.

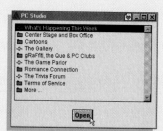

2 The PC Studio window opens. Click on What's Happening This Week (if necessary), and then click on Open.

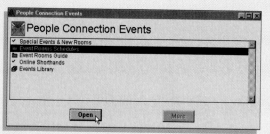

3 The People Connection Events window opens. To see the schedule of upcoming general events, click on Event Rooms schedules, and then click on Open.

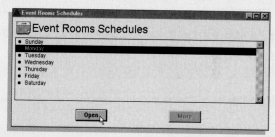

4 Another window opens, listing every day of the week. Click on the day you'd like to attend an event (if necessary), and then click on Open.

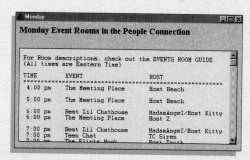

5 The next window lists your chosen day's events. Each listing includes a time, the event/room name, and the screen name of that event's on-line host or hosts. (An *online host*—not to be confused with the automated OnlineHost—is a live person who moderates events.)

6 To learn more about the event you plan to attend, return to the People Connection Events window, click on Event Rooms Guide, and then click on Open.

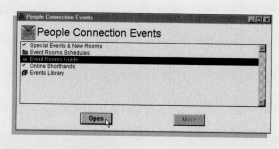

How to Participate in Center Stage Events

Center Stage is AOL's largest member gathering place, featuring new guests and events each week. The events in Center Stage include question and answer sessions, game shows, and other special events arranged by AOL.

Guests in this area range from actors to musicians to writers and even politicians. Unlike the member chat rooms which hold only 23 members, the Center Stage auditoriums can accommodate 5,000 members. Join in the fun, live on Center Stage.

▶ **1** Make sure you're signed on to AOL and click on People Connection in the Main menu. (Or click on the Flashbar's People Connection icon.)

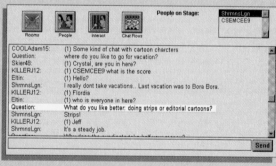

7 Your question or comment will soon appear in the discussion window.

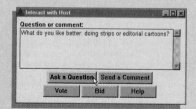

6 An Interact with Host window opens. Type your question or comment in the text box and then click on the Send a Question or Send a Comment button.

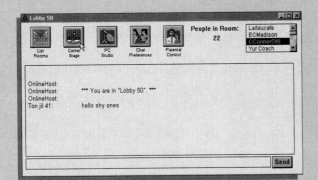

2 A Lobby window opens. Click on Center Stage.

3 The Center Stage window opens. Click on the icon representing the auditorium scheduled for your event. (If you're not sure which auditorium your event is in, first click on Today's Events.)

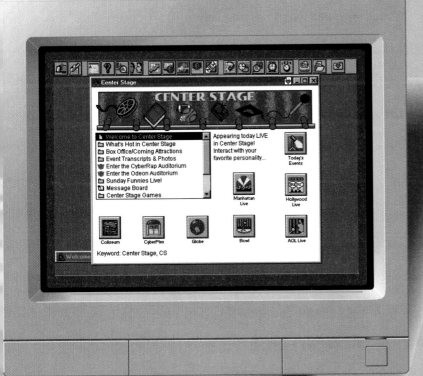

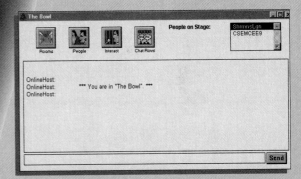

4 The auditorium window opens. The event's hosts are listed in the box on the upper right.

5 Once the event has started you'll see questions and comments for the host from other AOL members. To ask the host a question click on Interact.

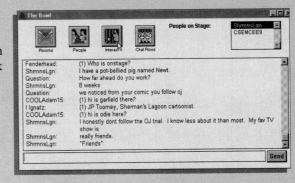

CHAPTER 24

Travel

 Whether it's for business or pleasure, travel can be hard work. Even before you leave home, you need to choose a destination, plan an itinerary, draft a travel budget, and make all the necessary reservations.

Fortunately, AOL can help simplify some of these details. Wherever you're going—a business trip to Raleigh, a family vacation to Disney World, or a weekend getaway to Toronto—AOL can help you get there and enjoy yourself once you arrive. This chapter introduces you to three AOL features devoted entirely to travel: EAAsy Sabre, Travelers' Corner, and the Travel Forum.

Think of EAAsy Sabre as your online travel agent. This comprehensive reservation system is the same one used by over 10,000 travel agencies. It enables you to research and even reserve airline flights, hotel rooms, and rental cars, directly from your computer.

If EAAsy Sabre is your online travel *agent*, then Travelers' Corner is your online travel *advisor*. Use it to choose an exciting destination or to learn more about a destination you've already selected. Whether your travel plans take you across the country or around the world, Travelers' Corner stands ready with valuable and insightful information.

The Travel Forum is for everyone who enjoys traveling. Use the resources in this area to plan your next trip or share your travel stories with other travelers.

How to Use EAAsy Sabre

If you've ever visited a travel agency in person, you've probably seen the clunky computer terminals that travel agents use to research and book airline flights and other travel reservations. Those terminals—and thousands like them—are all connected to EAAsy Sabre, a mammoth travel-reservation system that has been known to process over 250,000 reservations *in just one day*. Through a special computer connection known as a *gateway* between AOL and EAAsy Sabre, all the information and power of this reservation system can now be at your fingertips. This page shows you how to get started.

▶ **From the Reservation Menu mentioned in step 5, you can also research and reserve rental cars and hotel rooms. Just enter the appropriate number: 3 for rental cars or 4 for hotels.**

▶ **You can use EAAsy Sabre at any time to re-search travel arrangements, but before you can actually make any online reservations you must first complete an online registration application. To do this enter 7 on the EAAsy Sabre Reservation Menu, and the follow the on-screen instructions. Registration is free and immediate.**

▶ **EAAsy Sabre is not case sensitive. For exam-ple, even though EAAsy Sabre instructs you to type /EXIT to exit the system, you can also type /exit or /Exit to achieve the same results.**

▶ **Note the system navigation commands at the bottom of the EAAsy Sabre Reservation Menu shown in step 5. These commands are very useful if you get lost or need information while working with EAAsy Sabre.**

1 Make sure you're signed on to AOL and click on Travel in the Main menu. (Or click on the Flashbar's Keyword icon, use the keyword **eaasy sabre** and skip to step 3.)

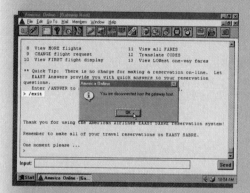

8 When you're done using EAAsy Sabre, type **/exit** or **/e**, click on Send, click on OK to close the dialog box shown here, and then close the Gateway Host window to return to AOL.

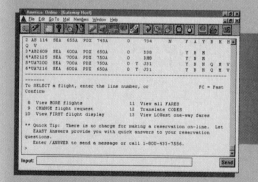

7 Once you've answered all the applicable questions, EAAsy Sabre displays a list of scheduled flights that most closely match your travel plans. From here, you can compare fares, pick the flight that best fits your plans and budget, and research return flights. You can't actually make flight reservations until you register to use EAAsy Sabre (see the second Tip on this page), but you can always print out the flight information and give it to your travel agent.

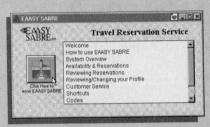

3 The EAAsy Sabre Travel Reservation Service window opens. Click on the Click Here button to Enter EAAsy Sabre.

2 The Travel window opens. Select EAAsy Sabre from the list box and double-click.

4 A Gateway Host window opens. You have just passed through the EAAsy Sabre gateway, and your computer is now communicating directly with the EAAsy Sabre system. Take your time, read each screen carefully, and you should find EAAsy Sabre fairly self-explanatory. Each screen displays some information, and then provides instructions on what type of information it needs from you. This screen, for example, advises you to press Enter (an alternative to clicking on Send) or to enter /**SIGNON**. The /SIGNON command is available only to people who have already registered to use EAAsy Sabre, so just click on Send or press Enter. (To make the text in this window easier to read, maximize the Gateway Host window.)

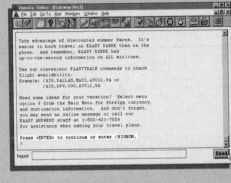

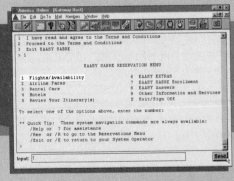

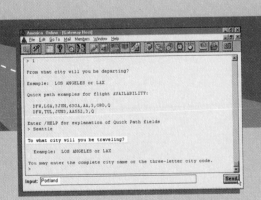

6 EAAsy Sabre asks you step-by-step questions about your travel plans, including city of departure, city of arrival, preferred airports (if applicable), and preferred travel date and time. Type in your answers to each of the questions presented, and click on Send after each answer.

5 After reading EAAsy Sabre's Terms and Conditions (something you should do before making any online reservations), you finally arrive at the EAAsy Sabre Reservation Menu. To start researching airline flights from here, type 1 for Flights/Availability and click on Send.

How to Use Travelers' Corner

Whether you've already made your travel plans or are still working on them, Travelers' Corner is a good place to learn more about any and all destinations. Developed and maintained by Weissmann Travel Reports, a major information provider to the travel industry, Travelers' Corner provides profiles on every state in the U.S. and on just about every country in the world. These concise, up-to-date profiles are alphabetically arranged so that you can quickly and easily find just the information you're seeking. This page shows you how to take a look at these profiles.

TIP SHEET

▶ If you prefer, you can also search for destinations by clicking on Search in step 3 rather than on an alphabetical group. For best results, search by state for U.S. destinations, and by country for international destinations.

▶ The online reports you see here are abridged from more detailed reports that are available in print. To order a printed report that you have to pay for, click on Order Travel Reports in the Travelers' Corner window. To get a free copy instead, visit a travel agent that carries Weissmann Travel Reports.

▶ Travelers' Corner also provides an Exotic Destinations Message Center (message board), an online version of the award-winning *Travel Holiday* magazine, and more. Explore the Travelers' Corner window to see what's available.

▶ Besides Travelers' Corner, AOL offers another separate travel-oriented area, the Travel Forum. To visit this area, use the keyword *travel forum* or *traveler*.

▶ **1** Make sure you're signed on to AOL and click on Travel in the Main menu. (Or click on the Flashbar's Keyword icon, use the keyword **travelers corner** and skip to step 3.)

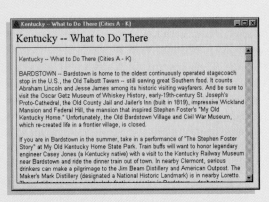

7 When you're done reading (or saving or printing) an article, close the article's window, and then repeat step 6 as desired to read other articles.

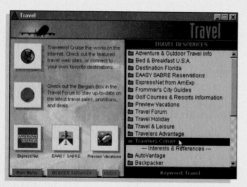

2 The Travel window opens. Scroll through the list box as necessary to select the Travelers' Corner item and double-click.

3 To start looking for the profile of a U.S. destination, click on United States Profiles. To start looking for the profile of an international destination, click on International Profiles.

4 If you clicked on United States Profiles in step 3, you'll see the U.S. Profiles window shown here. If you clicked on International Profiles, a similar International Profiles window opens. U.S. profiles are categorized by state; international profiles are categorized by country. To see a list of available states or countries, click the button for the appropriate alphabetical group.

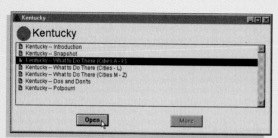

6 State and country profiles are divided into five article types: Introduction, Snapshot, What to Do There, Dos and Don'ts, and Potpourri. Each article details a different aspect of the state or country. To read one of the articles, click on the item and then click on Open.

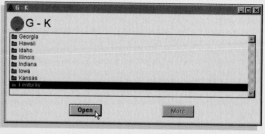

5 Another U.S. Profiles or International Profiles window opens. Scroll to find the desired state or country, and then click on Open.

How to Use the Travel Forum

A OL's Travel Forum is for everyone who enjoys traveling. The Travel Forum includes travel resources and message boards for members to exchange travel information and stories of their adventures.

You'll find practical advice on planning your vacation and how to save money on hotels and airfare. Plus traveling tips for travel in the U.S. and around the world. You can find out how to get the best exchange rates!

Start planning your next vacation on AOL!

1 Make sure you're signed on to AOL and click on Travel in the Main menu. (Or click on the Flashbar's Keyword icon, use the keyword **Travel Forum** and skip to step 3.)

7 Once you have opened a text window, scroll as necessary to read the document. To read more documents return to step 4.

► **Click on the Travel Books icon for news and reviews of travel books before you buy one. You can also order the books recommended here at a discount.**

► **Click on What's New and Events to find a calendar of events. AOL's guests include travel experts and authors who will be online in the Travel Cafe just to answer your travel questions.**

6 Move through the windows selecting items in the list box until you select an item with a file icon.

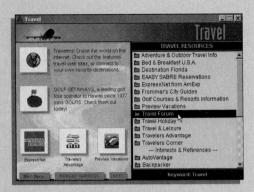

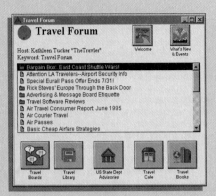

2 The Travel window opens. Scroll through the list box as necessary to select the Travel Forum item and double-click.

3 The Travel Forum window opens. The list box contains a wide variety of travel information for helping you plan your next trip. Use the icons to explore the Travel Forum's message boards, chat area, software library, and more.

4 Scroll through the list box as necessary to find an item that interests you, select the item and double-click.

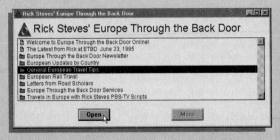

5 A new window opens displaying either text or another list box. If the window displays text, proceed to step 7. If the window displays a list box, scroll as necessary to find an item that interests you, select the item and click on Open.

CHAPTER 25

Marketplace

 Few communities, even electronic ones, are complete without shopping opportunities—and AOL provides plenty of ways to shop online.

You already know from Chapter 24 that you can reserve airline flights, hotel rooms, and rental cars online, but these are only a fraction of the shopping opportunities available in AOL's Marketplace department, a veritable mall of online stores.

Interested in discounts of up to 50 percent on over 250,000 brand name products? Look no further than Shoppers Advantage. Time to stock up on office supplies? OfficeMax Online probably has just what you need—and at discount prices. Tower Records is your online source for over 200,000 recordings. For the latest in computer hardware or software, check out Computer Express or PC Catalog. Have a big fight last night? Say "I'm sorry" with roses from the Flower Shop. AutoVantage Online helps you get the best possible price on a new car. And if you're just looking for a good old-fashioned book to read so that you can rest your screen-weary eyes, enjoy ten to 20 percent saving at the Online Bookstore.

Maybe mall shopping isn't your thing. Maybe you just need some extra cash or you're seeking or offering employment. If so, look into Classifieds Online, AOL's main area for member-to-member advertising.

So grab your wallet—we're going shopping!

How to Shop at an Online Store

With all the online stores that AOL has to offer, it's impossible to show them on just one page. Instead, we've chosen to introduce you to one store that should interest every AOL member: the AOL Online Store. Here, you can buy AOL paraphernalia to show off your community pride. Although every online store (unfortunately) works differently, this page will give you at least a taste of AOL online shopping.

▶ ❶ Make sure you're signed on to AOL and click on Marketplace in the Main menu.

❾ A new window opens. To place your order click on Place Order. Finally an Order Confirmation window opens. Click on Continue.

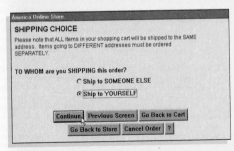

❽ A Shipping Choice window opens. Select the appropriate shipee and click on Continue. Use the next window (similar to the window in step 7) to enter the shipping address, then click on Continue .

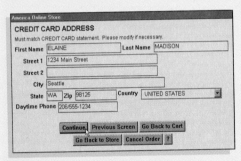

❼ A Credit Card Address window opens. If the information matches the information on your credit card statement, click on Continue. Otherwise, change the information as necessary, and then click on Continue.

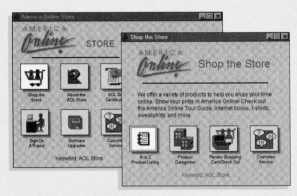

2 If a window entitled Marketplace Spotlight opens next, click on Marketplace (or close the window). The Marketplace window is now active, displaying a long list of on-line stores. Double-click on America Online Store.

3 The America Online Store window opens, click on Shop the Store. In the next window, click on A to Z Product Listing to see a list of available items.

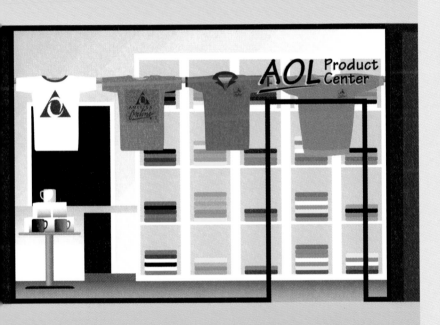

4 The A to Z Product Listing window opens, listing AOL sweat-shirts, T-shirts, and so on. Double-click on an item that interests you. The next window displays a picture and description of your selected item and its cost plus shipping and handling charges. To add the current item to your electronic shopping cart, click on the Click Here to Order button. Size (if applicable) and quantity windows will open to complete your order. (If you don't want to order the current item, click on Cancel.)

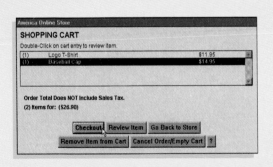

6 A Credit Card Information window opens. Fill in the text boxes with your credit card number, expiration date, and name as it appears on the card, and then click on Continue. As shown here, use no spaces, dashes, or slashes in the credit card number or expiration date.

5 Your Shopping Cart window displays the items in your electronic shopping cart and the total cost of those items. To order other items, click on Go Back to Store (you'll return to the A to Z Listing window shown in step 4). When you've selected all the items you want, click on Checkout.

How to Use Classifieds Online

Do you pore through your newspaper's classified ads, looking for good bargains on pre-enjoyed items? Do you have a garage, basement, or attic stuffed with possessions that you'll probably never use again, but that are just too valuable to throw or give away? Are you seeking a job or offering one? If you answered yes to any of these questions, then AOL's Classifieds Online area may be just the place for you. Classifieds Online comprises a set of AOL message boards (see Chapter 6) with the specific purpose of helping AOL members buy, sell, and trade old treasures and professional skills.

TIP SHEET

▶ **As with any classified ads, be careful when using them. Most AOL members are trustworthy, but the occasional one might try to cheat you.** Check out the Tradin' Talk board for recommended members and safe-trading tips. To access this board, double-click on Tradin' Talk (no ads) in the Classifieds Online window. (Trading tips are also available by clicking on the center button in this window.)

▶ **One of the few rules in Classifieds Online is that you must post your ad to the correct board, only to that board, and only once on that board.**

▶ **Each day, every topic is trimmed down to the 300 most recent ads.** This means that your ad may remain posted for only a day or so. Feel free to post your ad again once it's been removed.

▶ **For convenient access to classified ads located elsewhere on AOL, double-click on Other Ad Areas on AOL in the Classifieds Online window.**

1 Make sure you're signed on to AOL and click on Marketplace in the Main menu. (Or click on the Flashbar's Keyword icon, use the keyword **classifieds** and skip to step 3.)

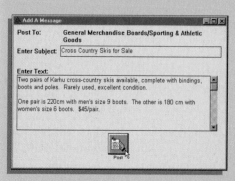

9 Type up your ad, making sure that the subject and message are as specific and detailed as possible, and then click on Post. Don't forget to check your e-mail frequently after posting an ad to see if you've received any responses.

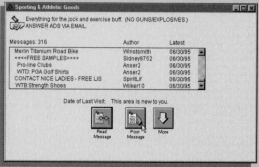

8 To post an ad of your own, click on Post Message. (Or click on Add Message if you're already reading an ad.)

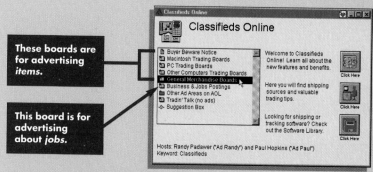

These boards are for advertising *items.*

This board is for advertising about *jobs.*

2 If a window entitled Marketplace Spotlight opens next, click on Marketplace (or close the window). The Marketplace window opens. Select Classifieds in the list box and double-click.

3 The Classifieds Online window opens. If you want to buy, sell, or trade an item, double-click on the most appropriate list box choice that contains the word Boards. If you're seeking or offering employment, double-click on Business & Job Postings, and then on Employment Offered or Wanted.

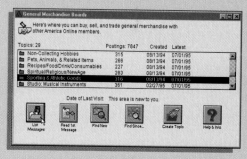

4 The next window lists the topics contained within your chosen board. Scroll as necessary, click on the most appropriate topic, and then click on List Messages.

5 The next window list the ads in your selected topic. To read an ad, scroll to find one that interests you (click on the More button as needed). Click on the ad and then on Read Message. If you want to post an ad of your own, skip to step 8.

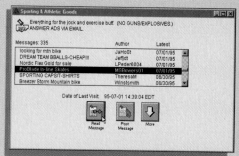

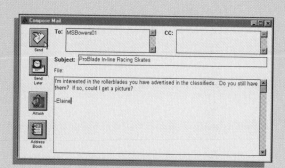

6 The next window displays the ad you selected. Read the ad to see if it describes what you want. If it doesn't, close the window and repeat step 5 to continue reading ads. (Or use the Previous Message or Next Message buttons to move directly from one ad to another.)

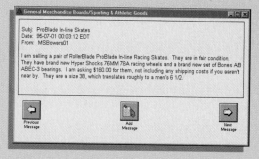

7 When you find an appealing ad, you can respond by e-mail to the advertiser. Later, check your e-mail for a response. (Do not post your reply on this message board; the advertiser may never see it there.)

CHAPTER 26

Internet Connection

Relatively unknown until recently, the *Internet* has become a household phrase.

Often cited as a model for the U.S. government's proposed "national information superhighway," the Internet is the world's largest interconnection, or *network*, of computers. Originally created by the U.S. government in the late 1960s for sharing information between research scientists and military personnel nationwide, the Internet has since grown exponentially. It now includes connections to research facilities, military installations, government offices, educational institutions, businesses, and online services worldwide. Through these connections, millions of people currently enjoy Internet access.

Although vast, widespread, and full of valuable information, the Internet suffers two major drawbacks: It can be difficult to connect to and even more difficult to use. Unlike AOL and other online services the Internet was not designed for the average computer user, but for the most computer literate. Adding to the confusion is that fact that no one actually *owns* the Internet, making it next to impossible to redesign the system for easier use.

Fortunately, AOL is working diligently to improve its easy-to-use connection to the Internet. Although the Internet is much too large and complex to cover in this one chapter, we will introduce you to some of its features: newsgroups, mailing lists, gopher, and the World Wide Web. (You already learned about the Internet's most popular feature, e-mail, in Chapter 7.)

How to Read a Newsgroup

Newsgroups—also known as *USENET groups, USENET news, Internet news,* and variations thereof—are the Internet's equivalent of AOL message boards (see Chapter 6), but on a world-wide scale. They contain online discussions rather than news. There are thousands upon thousands of available newsgroups, on topics ranging from dogs to volleyball to analyzing stock-market trends. With all these choices, it may seem an overwhelming task just to get started with newsgroups. For this reason, AOL already has set up a select list of newsgroups for you. On this page, you'll learn how to read one of these newsgroups.

1 Make sure you're signed on to AOL and click on Internet Connection in the Main menu. (Or click on the Flashbar's Keyword icon, use the keyword **newsgroups**, and skip to step 3.)

8 To jump directly to another subject within the current newsgroup, return to the group's subject window, click on the desired subject, and then on Read or List. To start reading another newsgroup, return to the Read My Newsgroups window, click on the desired group, and then on List Unread.

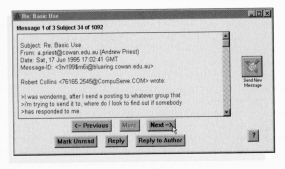

7 Another window opens, displaying your chosen message. When you've finished reading this message, click on Next to display the next message in your chosen category. Or, if you've already reached the current subject's last message, clicking on Next will display the first message in the next subject.

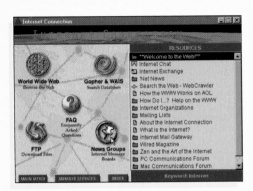

2 The Internet Connection window opens. Click on NewsGroups.

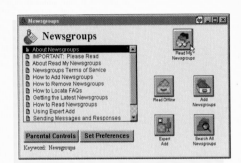

3 The Newsgroups window opens. Click on Read My Newsgroups.

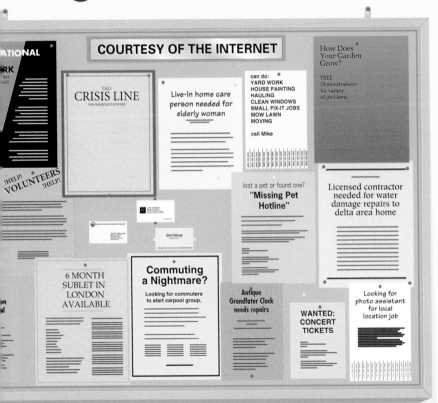

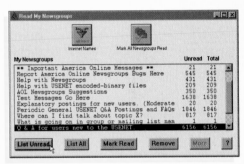

4 The Read My Newsgroups window opens, listing the newsgroups that AOL has set up for you, and the number of total and unread messages contained within each group. The newsgroups towards the top of this list are "local," shared only among AOL members, and have been created by AOL to help you learn about newsgroups. The remainder are true Internet Newsgroups, shared across the Internet. Click on any one of these groups, and then on List Unread.

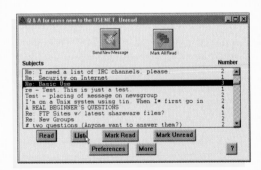

6 The next window you see lists your chosen subject's messages. Each listing contains the message sender's Internet address, and the date and time the message was posted. Click on a message, and then click on Read Message.

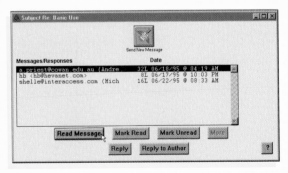

5 Another window opens, listing your chosen newsgroup's subjects and the number of messages contained within each subject. Click on a subject, and then click on List Messages. (To save a step and proceed directly to the selected subject's first message, you can click on Read instead, and then skip to step 7.)

How to Add a Newsgroup

Once you've read through the newsgroups that AOL has set up for you, you might want to start tapping into newsgroups that focus on particular topics that interest you, whether it be international politics or wine making. To facilitate this, you customize your Read My Newsgroups list by adding newsgroups to the list. Once you've added a newsgroup to this list, reading the group and posting messages to it are the same as for any of the newsgroups in your existing list. This page shows you how to add a newsgroup to your newsgroups list.

TIP SHEET

▶ **To review a newsgroup before adding it to your newsgroups list, click on List Subjects or Read Messages in step 4 before using the Add button.**

▶ **The Newsgroups window shown in step 1 provides two additional ways to add newsgroups to your list. If you know the exact Internet name for a newsgroup (perhaps you've read about it in another group), you can use the Expert Add button. To search for newsgroups, click on Search All Newsgroups. Or, to see the newest available newsgroups, click on Latest Newsgroups in the Add Newsgroups—Categories window shown in step 2.**

▶ **Be aware that Internet newsgroups are not subject to AOL's family-oriented terms of service, and might contain subject matter and language not suitable for everyone.**

▶ **To remove a newsgroup from your newsgroups list, click on the group in your Read My Newsgroups window, click on Remove, and then click on OK in the dialog box that follows.**

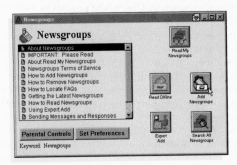

1 Open the Newsgroups window as described in steps 1 and 2 on the previous page, and then click on Add Newsgroups.

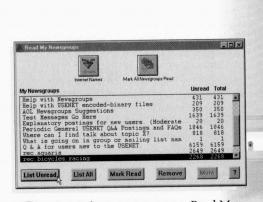

6 Now when you open your Read My Newsgroups window, your newly added newsgroup appears in the list. (This group might be displayed with a somewhat different name than what you click on in step 4.) You can now use the techniques described on the previous page to read and post messages in this group.

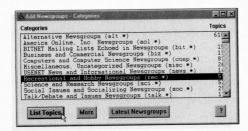

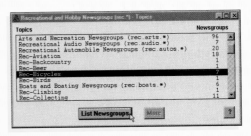

2 The Add Newsgroups - Categories window opens, listing the many available newsgroup categories and the number of topics contained within each category. Click on one of these categories, and then on List Topics.

3 The next window lists your chosen category's topics and the number of available newsgroups within each topic. Click on a topic, and then on List Newsgroups.

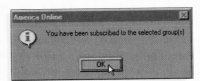

4 The next window lists your chosen topic's newsgroups and the number of messages within each group. If you see a newsgroup that you want to add to your customized list, click on that group, and then on Add.

5 A dialog box opens to inform you that you are now subscribed to the selected group.

How to Search for and Subscribe to a Mailing List

Like newsgroups, Internet *mailing lists* are topic-specific online discussion groups. The chief difference between newsgroups and mailing lists is how you gain access to these discussions. Rather than maintaining lists of messages, a mailing list exchanges messages through e-mail. To become part of a mailing list, you send e-mail to a specific e-mail address, requesting a *subscription* to that list. Within a few days, you'll start receiving in your AOL mailbox any messages that are sent to that mailing list. Once you become familiar with a particular mailing list, you, too, can start sending messages to everyone on that list.

TIP SHEET

▶ One of the drawbacks of subscribing to a mailing list is the 550-message limit in all your AOL mailboxes at any one time. Once you've reached 550, additional messages will not be added to your mail box; senders will receive a message that your mailbox is full. Although 550 may seem like a lot, some mailing lists can generate hundreds of messages per day. If you subscribe to one or more lists, check your mail regularly or use flash sessions to download your mail several times a day. Or check to see if the list has a digest option. Digests send you all of the mailing list's messages once or twice a day (as one message).

▶ If a mailing list generates more messages that you can handle, you might want to unsubscribe from the list. To do this, follow the instructions you got in step 4 or in step 6.

▶ Be aware that, like newsgroups, mailing lists might contain subject matter and language not suitable for everyone.

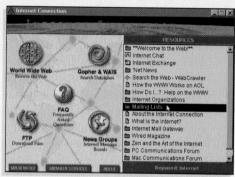

1 Make sure you're signed on to AOL, then select Internet Connection from the Main Menu to display the Internet Connection window. Double-click on Mailing Lists in the list box. (Or use the keyword **mailing lists**.)

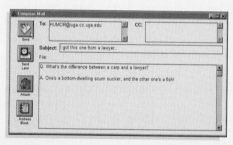

8 After reading enough messages to get a good feel for the topic, try sending your own message to the mailing list, by following the instructions you got in step 4 or have since received from the list.

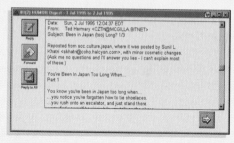

7 Shortly thereafter, depending on the list's popularity, you should start receiving messages from other list members. Here is an example.

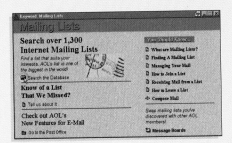

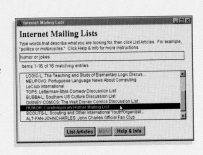

3 The Internet Mailing Lists search window opens. Use the techniques you learned in Chapter 11 to type in the search criteria. Then click on List Articles to display mailing lists that meet your criteria, and double-click on one of these lists.

2 The Mailing Lists window opens. Click on the Search the Database icon.

4 The next window that opens displays a description of your chosen mailing list, along with specific instructions for becoming part of that list. We maximized the window shown here so that you can see it better, but you should print your window's contents for reference.

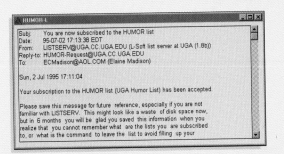

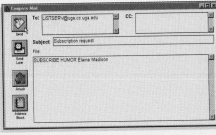

6 Every mailing list is different, but for most lists, you should receive fairly soon an e-mail message about your subscription request. If this message asks you to confirm your subscription, carefully follow the instructions for doing so. You may receive additional messages with instructions for appropriate message content, where to send messages, and so on.

5 To subscribe now to the mailing list you have displayed, compose and send an e-mail message, carefully following the subscription instructions from step 4. If your chosen list is maintained by a *list server* (an automated program that maintains the list), the instructions will tell you to type a short, specific command in the body of your message. If no command is specified, assume that your message is going to an actual person, and send a politely worded subscription request. (If you need help with e-mail, review Chapter 7.)

How to Use Gopher and WAIS

What's gopher? Unlike the small burrowing animal you may be thinking of, gopher is a tool for navigating the Internet with menus. Why gopher? gopher was originally developed at the University of Minnesota; the Golden Gopher is their mascot. Or maybe it's because gopher will "go for" you to get information from the Internet.

So what's WAIS? WAIS (pronounced like "ways") or Wide Area Information Server, is a means of searching through information on the Internet much like AOL uses Searchable Databases.

Gopher and WAIS paired together make an easy-to-use menu system with searching capabilities for browsing through the enormous amount of information on the Internet.

▶ **1** Make sure you're signed on to AOL and click on Internet Connection in the Main menu. (Or click on the Flashbar's Keyword icon, use the keyword **gopher**, and skip to step 3.)

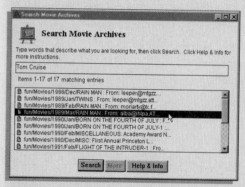

7 The lower text box will display all of the entries the search found which match your search criterion. Scroll through the list to find an item that interests you and double-click. If you do not find an item you're interested in, return to step 6 and redefine your search criterion.

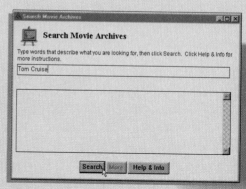

6 The WAIS search window looks much like the Searchable Database windows on AOL. Enter your search criterion in the top text box and click on Search.

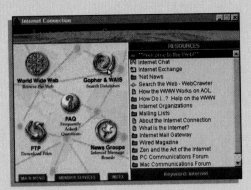

2 The Internet Connection window opens. Click on Gopher & WAIS.

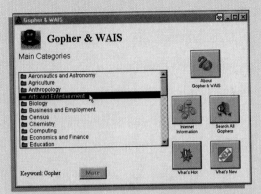

3 The main gopher menu opens. Double-click on one of the categories listed to begin "burrowing" for information.

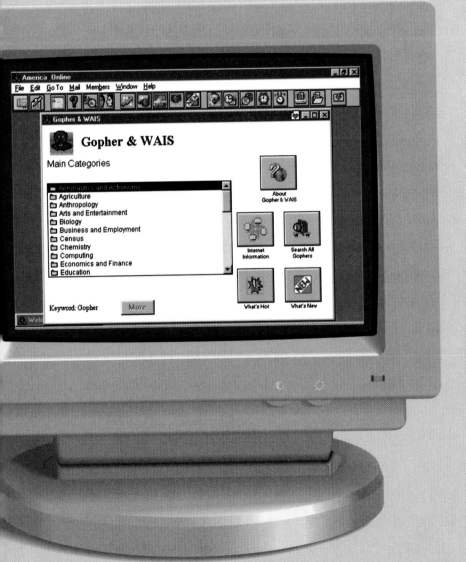

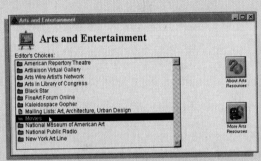

4 If you selected a menu item with a folder icon another menu will open. If you selected a menu item with a file icon a text window will open.

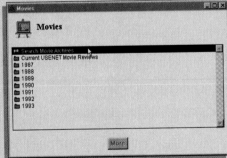

5 As you move through the gopher menus discovering more menus and information you may find an item with an open book icon. The open book icon represents a WAIS search database. Click on the item to open a search window.

How to Browse the World Wide Web

The World Wide Web (WWW) is a vast resource of business, personal, government, educational, and entertainment information. WWW information is found in many different forms, including text, graphics, video, and even sound—all easily accessible with the use of a "browser."

WWW browsers are user-friendly tools which allow you to navigate the Internet just by clicking your mouse. With new pages and sites being added daily you'll never run out of places to visit on the WWW.

The WWW browser has more features than we can cover in just one page so we'll introduce you to the browser and then let you explore its other features on your own.

▶ **1** Make sure you're signed on to AOL and click on Internet Connection in the Main menu.

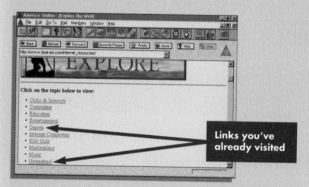

Links you've already visited

7 When you click on the Back button the page you viewed previously is displayed. Note that the links which you have previously selected have changed color. This is the browser's way of helping you keep track of where you've been.

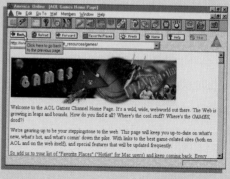

6 Another new page is displayed for you to read and follow; click on the links that interest you. To return to the previous page, click on the Back button.

TIP SHEET

▶ **Many AOL departments include links to Internet sites. Clicking on an item designated as an Internet site will bring up a WWW browser window and load the appropriate page.**

▶ **You'll often find references to web sites listed as URLs (Uniform Resource Locators) or "http," for example "http://gnn.com." To access these Web sites, open the AOL Web browser, use your mouse to delete the URL in the text box, type in the new URL and press Enter. Make sure you type the URL exactly as given to you, paying close attention to upper- and lowercase characters.**

▶ **URLs always use the forward slash (/), not the backslash (\) commonly used in DOS.**

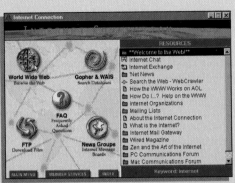

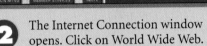

AOL browser toolbar

URL text box

2 The Internet Connection window opens. Click on World Wide Web.

3 The AOL web home page opens. You're now in the WWW browser. The AOL WWW browser includes a toolbar with eight buttons to assist you while browsing. Hold your mouse over each button for a "balloon" explaining the purpose of the button. (For easier reading, maximize the WWW home page window as shown here.)

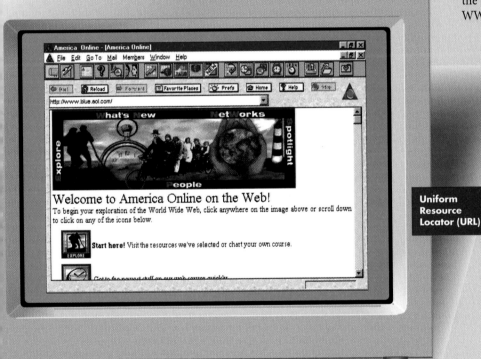

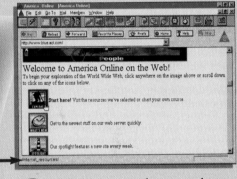

Uniform Resource Locator (URL)

4 WWW pages are hypertext documents; clicking on a link will take you to other pages. Links may be text or images: Text links appear underlined and in color; image links are outlined in color and when you point to them with your mouse, you'll see a URL at the bottom of the screen. Click on one of the links in this page.

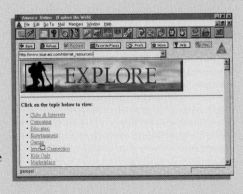

5 A new page is displayed. You'll notice the AOL icon turns as the page is being loaded. This tells you that the browser is working. (If you decide not to load the page, click on the Stop button.) Double-click on one of the links that interests you.

APPENDIX

Goodbye!

 Congratulations! Having read this far, you now should be a comfortable, confident AOL member, ready to find online information with a minimum of effort, time, and expense. We hope that this book will continue to serve as a handy reference guide for all your future AOL explorations.

As a reward for your accomplishment, we're leaving you with a gift: some bonus tips that will help you use AOL and AOL for Windows even more efficiently.

Read on and learn.

Bonus Tips

As we produced this book, we came up with several useful tips that really didn't fit anywhere else in the book. Many of those tips are listed here. Although these suggestions certainly aren't crucial to your success in using AOL, they can save you some effort and online time, as well as help you make AOL work the way *you* want it to.

1. Escape from the hourglass. When you open an online window, it can take from several seconds to several minutes for that window's information to travel from AOL to your computer. In the meantime, your mouse pointer changes to an hourglass, indicating that you should wait. In most cases, the hourglass will disappear immediately, indicating that you can now close this window and continue on to other tasks. But if the window's information isn't something you're interested in anyway and you don't want to wait, you can stop the information flow by pressing the Escape key or by choosing Stop Incoming Text from the File menu. If the window contains information that you do want to read, you can go ahead and start scrolling while the hourglass is still visible.

2. Log text. Rather that reading text online, or manually saving or printing text from individual online windows, you can instead automatically capture, or log, the text from every window you open. This text moves directly into a disk file, which you can then open and read after you sign off. To learn more about the File, Logging command, consult offline help. (See Chapter 5 for information on using offline help.)

3. Working with text you've saved. Once you've saved or logged text to a disk, you can view, edit, and even print that text from within AOL for Windows. To do this, choose Open from the File menu, click on the file's name, and then click on OK. Text that you've saved to disk can also be opened with many other Windows applications, including Notepad, Write, and many popular word processing programs.

4. Working with a downloaded image. Besides viewing an image as you download it, you can also redisplay that image with AOL for Windows. To do so, use the File, Open command as described in the previous tip. You can also view many downloaded images using some other Windows applications, including Paintbrush.

5. Use the Windows Clipboard. The Windows Clipboard enables you to transfer text quickly and easily from one AOL window to another, from AOL for Windows to other Windows applications, and from other Windows applications to AOL for Windows. You can use the Clipboard for thousands of purposes—from copying a complex e-mail address to using a word processing program for spell-checking your outgoing mail messages. To use the Clipboard, select (drag across) the text you want to transfer, choose either Cut or Copy from the Edit menu, position the insertion point wherever you want to place the text, and then choose Paste from the File menu. To learn more about the Windows Clipboard, consult your Windows documentation.

6. Create your own window. Choose New from the File menu to open a blank window in which you can type text. You can save quite a bit of online time by typing text in one of these windows when you're off line, and then using the Clipboard to transfer the text to an online window.

7. Avoid AOL when it's slow. As you've worked with AOL, you may have discovered that the service works very quickly at some times, and very slowly at others. This is affected by how many members are signed on to AOL at the time: the more members on line, the slower the system. To save yourself some online charges, especially when you're downloading files, avoid AOL during its peak times of evenings and weekends.

8. Accept that some windows just don't close. You may have discovered that some online windows, such as the online Welcome! window, never actually close. You can *minimize* the window, or you can *hide* it by entering a free area, but you can't close it. Don't waste your time worrying about it.

9. Set your preferences. Use the Members, Preferences command to change the way AOL for Windows works overall. For example, you can tell AOL for Windows to automatically scroll windows as they fill with text, and you can have AOL for Windows automatically notify you when a member enters or leaves your current chat room. You may also want to set your WWW preferences, especially if you're using a slow modem.

10. Explore Members Helping Members. For hundreds of additional AOL tips from fellow members, take some time to peruse the Members Helping Members message board. Click on Members Help Members in Your Online Help Center (See Chapter 5), or use the keyword **mhm**. If you have a valuable tip of your own, be sure to post it on this board so that other members can benefit from it.

INDEX